TREASURES OF
Caribbean
KITCHEN

ANNE-MARIE WHITTAKER

CARIBBEAN

Macmillan Education
Between Towns Road, Oxford OX4 3PP
A division of Macmillan Publishers Limited
Companies and representatives throughout the world

www.macmillan-caribbean.com

ISBN-13 : 978-0333-73779-8
ISBN-10 : 0-333-73779-2

Text © Anne-Marie Whittaker 1999
Design and illustration © Macmillan Publishers Limited 1999

First published 1999

Designed by Stafford & Stafford, Uffington
Illustrations by Martin Saunders
Cover Design by Stafford & Stafford, Uffington
Cover Illustrations by Martin Saunders

Printed and bound in Thailand

2010 2009 2008 2007 2006
13 12 11 10 9 8 7 6 5

DEDICATION

To John and Buddie Leib, for their love and support throughout the years.

CONTENTS

CONTENTS

CONTENTS

PREFACE

When you think of the Caribbean, it usually conjures up visions of tropical sunsets, lazy laid-back days, rum punches, warm temperatures and hot spicy foods.

Now: when you think of that hot spicy food, you probably believe that it tastes the same wherever you go. However, this couldn't be further from the truth.

You see, Caribbean cooking is like the Caribbean itself – while there is a common cultural thread that defines the Caribbean identity, each island is so different from the other, that by travelling just 128 miles you leave the island of Barbados with its typically-English atmosphere and end up in totally-French Martinique. As you continue your journey, you can't help but be amazed at the differences, different dialects – (to the point where a judge in Grenada ordered an interpreter for a witness from a neighbouring island), different landscapes – from flat coral islands with white sandy beaches and clear water to very mountainous islands, some with still active volcanoes.

The cultural differences are a direct result of the colonisation of the islands by various colonial powers at some point in their history and the blending of those French, Spanish, English, Dutch and Portuguese cultures with the African, Indian and Chinese influences which were introduced either with the slaves or the indentured servants. In some countries we even had the indigenous Amerindian population to add to the mix. Some islands were colonised by several European powers in the course of their history, in the days when the only real entertainment for the population was to engage in a good old-fashioned war. This, more than anything else, makes it very difficult to identify a singular Caribbean style of cooking and, even more so, a true Caribbean cook.

While we are on the subject of the islands, let's not forget Guyana, which is very much a part of the Caribbean although it is located on the mainland of South America, for it is here that six different cultures influenced the final blend ... so here we can enjoy anything from a good Pepperpot, which is an Amerindian creation made from a poisonous root, to a very spicy Curry, straight from the heart of India.

I consider myself very fortunate to have been born in this region. I was born in Guyana and spent a good part of my life in Barbados and Trinidad. My keen interest in cooking made it all the more interesting. Wherever I lived, my first order of business was to find out 'what's cooking?' Over the years, I have perfected the many cooking techniques from these countries and have visited several other islands where I always made it a point to find out the whys and wherefores of the local dishes.

Because Caribbean people do not dine out as a rule, the authentic foods of the region are almost never found in restaurants and, when they are, they are usually a corruption of the real thing, just to accommodate the typical taste of the average visitor. It is only when you visit a local home that the true culture of Caribbean cooking is revealed. But, you have to be fortunate enough to be invited in the first place! If you aren't, the next best thing is to take a drive through a village on Sunday morning and enjoy the varying smells of highly-seasoned foods which permeate the atmosphere, for tradition dictates that Sunday lunch is the most special meal of the week, when all the family gathers to spend some 'quality time' together.

Treasures of my Caribbean Kitchen represents a collection of recipes that captures the essence of our food and our way of life, both of which I totally enjoy. It is my sincere hope that this book will take your tastebuds on an exciting Caribbean adventure.

ABOUT THE AUTHOR

Anne-Marie Whittaker was born in Guyana. She spent many of her growing-up years in Barbados where she now lives with her husband and two children. Her many careers include secretary, sales representative, businesswoman, publisher and homemaker. But most of all she loves entertaining and cooking – so much so that she has been nicknamed 'The Mighty Entertainer' by her friends.

Anne-Marie is an entrepreneur who has owned and managed a computer store and restaurants as well as successfully completing several publishing projects: however, if you ask anyone about her, the first thing that comes to mind is her cooking and entertaining. Life in the Caribbean is like one big holiday and she is forever being called upon to organise parties and give advice on preparing tasty dishes. She has also developed quite a following for **her exotic Caribbean creations – Gourmet Sauces,** which are manufactured in Barbados and sold in the United States, England, Canada and the Caribbean under the *Native Treasures* label.

She believes firmly that in the world of 'Hot and Spicy' cuisine, the Caribbean, with its wide variety of cultures, is second to none.

ACKNOWLEDGEMENTS

Working on this book has truly been a labour of love. The love of the Caribbean, our people and, more precisely, our food.

It has been my good fortune to be surrounded by friends who took the time to support and encourage me along the way . . .

My sincere thanks to Kim and Mark Trotman who were my 'guinea pigs' on more occasions than I can count. I will never forget the day I was experimenting with bananas and rice – the flavours did not come together as I had hoped and the smell in my kitchen was more reflective of the cat having an accident than a mouth-watering spread. True to form, they first 'fired a grog' and then we all laughed our heads off.

Words alone cannot express my appreciation for the effort made by my good friend Jeffrey Evanson who kept me motivated and went to great lengths to explain the 'Law Of Attraction'. When two bodies of equal mass are moving towards each other at a given speed, as the distance between them decreases, the speed increases. He is convinced that when things start to happen, it all comes in a rush!

Thank you to Ruth Jordan and Denis Wilkie, who reminded me of the principles of instalments - that you can produce quite a lot with very little, if you just take your time.

Thanks to Jasmine and Frank Butcher for believing in the cuisine and the recipes. Over the years we have spent many enjoyable hours planning menus for parties and entertaining.

Thanks to Ena Harvey for lending a listening ear and for her much appreciated advice.

Thanks too are due to that all-capable – all-Barbadian – chef, Anthony Johnson, whose food styling talents and skill can be enjoyed and appreciated by taking a look at the photos that follow . . .

My heartfelt thanks to Andrea and Noel Duguid (my partners in *Native Treasures*) who never gave up on the dream of one day seeing our Gourmet Sauces go international.

Luck was also on my side . . . in 1995 it was my good fortune to meet a man by the name of Dan Kennedy at a seminar in Chicago. I already knew about his work and was even putting into practice some of his principles; however, that meeting opened an entirely new world, and for that I am very grateful.

None of this would ever have come to pass without the magnificent effort made by my husband, Charlie, and the support of our children, Tiffany and Tristan. The tremendous focus necessary to bring this project together was made possible by my 'support team'. They gave me the encouragement, time and space needed to get the mass of information out of my head and down on paper. I did not realise just how much work was involved until I started. It is very easy for me to tell stories and cook the dishes but the challenge came when it had to be documented in black and white . . . To Charlie, a special 'Thank You' for his help with the research and so much more. I have always been told it is often difficult for husbands and wives to work as a team and I feel truly blessed to have a husband like Charlie who not only supports my 'adventures' but will work tirelessly to make them happen.

COOKING TIPS

Baking	Keep your oven clean. The build up of grease absorbs the heat and this can change your baking temperature.
	Place baking pans in the centre of the oven.
	To settle the mixture in a baking tin, lift and drop it firmly on a hard surface.
	Cover cake with a thick sheet of paper for the first 30 minutes of baking. Cut slits in the paper to allow the steam to escape. This helps to prevent cracking.
	When melting chocolate, first coat the inside of the pan with a layer of oil.
Beans	To remove excess gas from beans, soak them overnight in water mixed with one teaspoon of baking soda.
BBQ	When grilling on the Bar-B-Q, grease the grill before and during cooking to prevent the meat from sticking.
Browning	Wet meat will not brown, so dry it first with paper towel.
Crackling	To make pork skin really crackling, score the fat and rub it with salt, oil and black pepper. Bake in a very hot oven (450 °F) for 30 minutes then reduce heat and roast slowly until done.
Curry	Curry powder imparts its flavour better if stir-fried first.
Eggs	To test for bad eggs, place in a bowl with water. Fresh eggs will sink and bad ones will rise.
Fat	To remove fat from the surface of soups and stews, quickly wipe over the surface with a pastry brush or clean absorbent kitchen towel.
Fish	Fish flakes easily when done. Do not overcook.
	When shallow-frying fish, cook skin side last.
	To recognise fresh fish, look for clear and bulging eyes. The scales and flesh should also be firm to the touch.
Herbs	When the recipe calls for dried herbs and you want to substitute fresh, double the quantity.
Roasting	For juicy, tender roasts, bake uncovered in a very hot oven (450 °F) for 30 minutes. Turn to brown all the sides, then reduce heat, cover and cook slowly until done.
Rice	Soak rice in water for two hours before cooking. This rehydrates the rice and it cooks faster in less liquid. Do not uncover the pan and stir the rice while it is cooking. It is the steam that makes the rice light and fluffy.
Soups	Soups should be simmered, not boiled. Boiling destroys the nutrients.
	If soup is too salty, add some chopped raw potato. Remove the potato just before serving.
Tenderising	When tenderising meat with a mallet, dip it each time into cold water first. This prevents the meat from breaking up and splitting.
	The acid in marinades helps to tenderise meat. The best containers to use are glass or stainless steel.

CONVERSION TABLES

WEIGHTS

US	METRIC
1 oz	30 g
2 oz	60 g
3 oz	90 g
4 oz/¼ lb	125 g
5 oz	155 g
6 oz	185 g
8 oz/½ lb	250 g
12 oz/¾ lb	375 g
16 oz/1 lb	500 g
2 lb	1000 g/1 kg

oz – ounce
lb – pound
g – gram
kg – kilogram

LIQUIDS

METRIC	US	UK
30 ml	2 tbs	1 fl. oz
60 ml	¼ cup	2 fl. oz
80 ml	⅓ cup	3 fl. oz
125 ml	½ cup	4 fl. oz
160 ml	⅔ cup	5 fl. oz
180 ml	¾ cup	6 fl. oz
250 ml	1 cup/½ pt	8 fl. oz
375 ml	1½ cups	12 fl. oz
500 ml	2 cups/1 pt	16 fl. oz
1000 ml/1 litre	4 cups/1qt/2 pt	32 fl. oz

ml – millilitre
fl. oz – fluid ounce
tbs – tablespoon
qt – quart
pt – pint

Note: All values are approximate

1 stick of margarine = ½ cup = 113 grams

OVEN TEMPERATURES

Gas mark	¼	2	4	6	8
Fahrenheit (°F)	225	300	350	400	450
Celsius (°C)	110	150	180	200	230

INGREDIENTS

MSG = Monosodiumglutamate (*Accent*, if possible)
Bassa Bassa Sauce – see page 47 for Tamarind Sauce, if Bassa Bassa Sauce not available

soup

BLACK BEAN SOUP

This delicious soup is Spanish in origin and comes from the island of Cuba.

INGREDIENTS

1 lb black beans *soaked in water overnight, or* 2 cans (16 oz) canned variety

10 cups water

6 cloves garlic *minced*

1 large onion *diced*

1 tbs seasoned salt

4 oz smoked sausage *sliced*

1 oz cilantro *finely chopped*

1 large green pepper *seeded and chopped*

¼ Scotch bonnet or habanero pepper *chopped*

2 tbs roasted ground cumin

2 tbs oregano

1 tsp thyme

1 whole orange

12 whole cloves

Serves 6

METHOD

Wash and drain the beans, then place them in a stockpot with the water, onion, garlic and seasoned salt. Bring to the boil, reduce heat and simmer for 1 hour, or until the beans are tender. Remove a quarter of the beans to a blender and purée them.

Return the purée to the pot and add the smoked sausage, cilantro, green pepper, hot pepper, cumin, oregano and thyme. Stick the cloves into the orange and lower this also into the pot. Bring to the boil, reduce heat and simmer for 30 minutes.

Remove orange before serving.

(See **Note** on page 33 re cooking peas/beans.)

Black Bean Soup

BLACKEYE PEAS SOUP

Soup always warms the soul and this one is no exception. The blackeye peas and coconut milk are a classic example of the blending of the many cultures that exist in the Caribbean, in this case African and Asian respectively.

INGREDIENTS

1 cup blackeye peas *soaked in water overnight, or* 1 can (16 oz) canned variety

10 oz ham *cut into cubes*

2 medium onions *chopped*

1 tbs sugar

2 tomatoes *peeled and chopped*

2½ cups coconut milk

½ oz fresh thyme

½ oz fresh basil

½ oz fresh marjoram

¼ tsp Scotch bonnet or habanero pepper *minced*

½ cup rum

1 tbs vegetable oil

1 bay leaf

salt *to taste*

Serves 4

METHOD

Tie the herbs together.

Wash and drain the peas, then place in a stockpot with the ham and about 6 cups water. Add the bay leaf, herbs, sugar and half of the onion and bring to the boil. Cover the pot and simmer until the peas and ham are tender. Remove the ham, herbs and bay leaf from the stock. Discard the seasonings and reserve the ham.

Heat the oil in a pan and sauté the remaining onion for about 5 minutes. Next add the tomatoes and cook for a few minutes, stirring constantly. Transfer this to the main pot, add the coconut milk and pepper and simmer for 10 minutes.

Purée in a blender and return to the pot, adding the rum and reserved ham. Adjust seasonings to taste, and simmer for 5 minutes.

(See **Note** on page 33 re cooking peas/beans.)

BOUILLON

This soup comes from St Lucia and is a favourite with both young and old. The dumplings are always the centre of attention – some cooks make them into different shapes in an effort to make the meal more exciting for the children.

INGREDIENTS

2 cups red kidney beans *soaked overnight, or* 4 cups canned variety

2 lb eddoes (tarro) *peeled and sliced 1 inch thick*

2 lb cured pig-tails *soaked in boiling water overnight*

1 large onion *chopped*

8 cloves garlic *minced*

½ tsp marjoram

½ tsp thyme

½ tsp basil

½ tsp oregano

2 celery stalks *chopped*

2 oz fresh cilantro (coriander) *chopped*

½ tsp habanero *or* Scotch bonnet pepper *minced*

½ cup margarine

salt *to taste*

14 cups water

Dumplings

2 cups flour

1 tbs sugar

½ tsp salt

1 tsp baking powder

½ cup water

Serves 8

METHOD

Place the kidney beans in a large stockpot with the water, onion, garlic, herbs, cilantro, celery and pepper. Bring to the boil, reduce heat and simmer for 15 minutes.

In the meantime, drain the pig-tails, place in another saucepan with water and boil for 15 minutes.

Chop the tails into 1 inch pieces and add to the stockpot together with the eddoes. Continue to cook for another 20 minutes, then add the dumplings.

Adjust the salt to your taste, stir in the margarine and simmer for 15 minutes more.

To make the dumplings...

Mix all of the ingredients together and knead on a floured board for 4 minutes. Add a little water if necessary. Form into balls about 1 inch in diameter

Some of the dumplings can also be shaped like discs about the size of a quarter and some like your little finger.

Add to the soup about 15 minutes before the end.

(See **Note** on page 33 re cooking peas/beans.)

Note:

In some islands, dumplings are made with baking powder and sugar and in others it is taboo to use those two ingredients. The two versions are known as 'floaters' and 'sinkers' respectively. As a matter of fact whenever a Barbadian and a Jamaican get involved in a 'dumpling' conversation, it can get quite heated over which version is the best. For many people 'dumplings' are sacred.

My little son Tristan's face lights up at the mention of having soup with dumplings for dinner. In many households, the person to remove the last dumpling from the pot is not treated very kindly and to make soup without dumplings is a 'waste of time'. I hope this explains how passionately Caribbean people feel about their dumplings and the integral role they play in our cuisine!

CALLALOO SOUP WITH CRAB

Callaloo Soup with Crab

This tasty dish comes from the Island of the Hummingbird – Trinidad, but it is also made in Guyana. As a child I would spend hours cracking and sucking the crab from the shell. It was great fun.

Sunday was the most popular time for preparing this dish because the land crabs could be bought fresh in the open-air market early in the morning. Also, it is quite normal to sit for two hours at the dinner table removing every last piece of meat from the shells.

In this recipe, you can use crab meat that has already been removed from the shell, if whole crabs are not available.

In St Vincent, one of the very popular wayside foods is Boiled Corn and they use Callaloo Soup as the base in which to boil the corn. It is truly delicious! The other unique feature about this wayside specialty is how it is served. After cooking the soup/corn is allowed to cool a little and then sold to the public in plastic bags. An ear of corn is placed in the bag followed by a ladle of soup. The top of the bag is tied and away you go!

The crabs and shrimp can be deleted from this recipe when making Boiled Corn.

INGREDIENTS

3 oz salt pork

8 oz crab meat *or* 6 whole crabs
    that have been scrubbed clean

10 oz frozen *or* fresh spinach
    (callaloo)

8 okras

3 cloves garlic *minced*

1 green onion *chopped*

1 onion *diced*

1½ tbs mixed herbs (oregano,
    thyme, marjoram, basil)

3 tbs cilantro (coriander) *minced*

seasoned salt *to taste*

½ tsp MSG (optional)

minced habanero *or* Scotch bonnet
    pepper *to taste*

9 cups water

1 can (16 ozs) coconut milk

4 oz peeled shrimp

2 oz margarine

Serves 6

METHOD

Soak salt pork in hot water for about 1 hour, then cut up into small pieces.

Put all the ingredients expect the crab meat, shrimp and margarine into a saucepan and bring to the boil. Simmer for about 30 to 45 minutes.

Purée with hand blender or swizzle. Add crabs or crab meat, margarine and shrimp and continue to simmer for another 20 minutes.

Serve hot.

CONCH

Conch, or lambi, as it is known in the French islands and former French colonies, is one of the more popular Caribbean sea foods. It is a snail-like creature that exists in a beautiful pink shell which may be quite large. It is born as larva and floats freely in the water until its shell develops and weighs it down to the sand. In St Lucia, the lambi is harvested using scuba equipment, and brought inshore, where it is kept alive in undersea cages. When purchased fresh, the vendor rows out to his cages and stacks his boat with live conch in the shell. It is then brought to shore, where the shell is punched at its apex and a sharp knife used to force out the conch. Once it is out, the conch is weighed, cleaned by cutting away unwanted parts and then washed in sea water.

Conch is usually very tough and must be cooked for an hour and a half before it becomes soft enough to eat; however if you ask the vendor to 'pound it', it will be tenderised with the aid of a large piece of wood or a hammer and then takes only 15 minutes to cook.

A conch can also be forced from its shell by gradually bringing it to the boil. The shell is preserved using this method. It is then cleaned and highly polished to make beautiful table lamps, clocks and other decorative items.

In St Lucia, the Bahamas, the Cayman Islands and Belize you can go into almost any restaurant and find conch on the menu. Its popularity may be due in part to its alleged properties as an aphrodisiac.

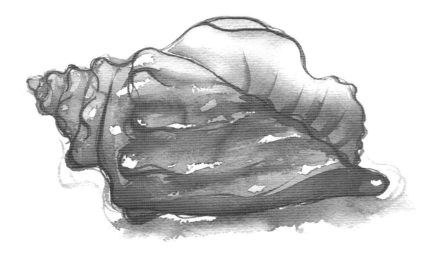

CONCH CHOWDER

Places like the Bahamas, Cayman and Belize have made this soup very popular. On your next visit try some, it is readily available in many restaurants. On a cold winter's day, make up a batch of this soup and be instantly 'transported' to the sunshine …

INGREDIENTS

¼ cup vegetable oil

1 lb conch meat

1 large lemon

2 stalks celery

5 cloves garlic *minced*

1 large onion *diced*

1 green pepper *seeded and diced*

5 cups water

3 green plantains *or* green bananas
peeled and sliced

1 tbs seasoned salt

1 cup evaporated milk

½ cup coconut milk

1 tbs ground allspice

Scotch bonnet *or* habanero pepper
to taste, chopped

1 tsp grated nutmeg

3 tbs cornstarch *if required* (see
Note)

Serves 4

METHOD

Wash the conch and squeeze the juice of the lemon on it. Leave it to stand for 5 minutes, then pound the meat with a mallet to soften. Wash again and cut into ½ inch cubes. Season with the onion, garlic and seasoned salt.

Heat the oil in a stockpot and sauté the conch for about 5 minutes, stirring constantly. Add the green pepper, hot pepper and celery, and continue to cook for a further 5 minutes.

Next, add the water and plantains and cook until the conch and plantains are tender, (approximately 30 minutes). Purée with a hand blender. Pour in the evaporated milk, coconut milk, allspice and nutmeg, and simmer for 15 minutes.

Note:
If the soup is not thick enough mix the cornstarch with a little water and add to the pot. Continue to simmer for another 5 minutes.

COWHEEL AND BARLEY SOUP

Guyana and Belize lay claim to this one. Like Mannish Water from Jamaica and Goat Water from St Vincent, this soup is supposed to put 'lead in your pencil.' The men swear by it!

INGREDIENTS

2 lb cowheel *cut into 1½ inch rounds*

1 onion *sliced*

4 cloves garlic *minced*

½ Scotch bonnet pepper

2 tsp seasoning salt

10 cups water

3 carrots *sliced*

½ tsp thyme

½ tsp marjoram

1½ cups barley

Serves 6

METHOD

Wash the cowheel and place in a stockpot with the water, seasoning salt, onion, garlic and pepper. Bring to the boil, then reduce heat and simmer for 1 hour. Skim off the foam as it rises to the top.

After 1 hour add the barley, carrots, thyme and marjoram. Continue to simmer for a further hour. Add more water if necessary and adjust seasonings to taste.

The meat should fall off the bones when it is finished.

CREOLE PUMPKIN SOUP

This soup is made on many of the Caribbean islands. However, this recipe is the version from Barbados where it is also known as 'Long Soup'. Some cooks even use coconut water as the base liquid instead of regular water.

Some years ago I founded the 'Caribbean Soup Boilers Association'. It all started when some friends were coming from Guyana to visit us at Easter. I wanted to have a party with a difference and after much thought decided to make a huge pot of soup (about 15 gallons). We lit a bonfire outside the house and cooked the soup outdoors. The guests were invited to make a contribution to the pot and that night 'soup boiled like never before'. Everyone enjoyed the party so much that when my friends went back to Guyana they introduced their friends to it and now the tradition has spread to a few other islands in the Caribbean.

INGREDIENTS

2 cups diced pumpkin *or* butternut squash

2 onions *diced*

2 oz salt pork

3 cloves garlic *minced*

1 cup ham *cubed*

1 cup yellow split peas *washed*

8 oz beef *cubed*

2 carrots *peeled and sliced*

2 cups cabbage *sliced with heart removed*

2 large potatoes *peeled and diced*

1 medium yam *peeled and diced*

1 medium sweet potato *peeled and diced*

1 tsp thyme

1 tsp basil

1 tsp marjoram

seasoned salt *to taste*

enough water to cover vegetables

Dumplings
Note: see page 4

Serves 6

METHOD

Place all of the ingredients into a large saucepan or pressure cooker and add enough water to cover the vegetables.

Cook for 1 hour 15 minutes, or 30 minutes if using a pressure cooker.

Meanwhile, make the dumplings and add to the soup 15 minutes before the end of cooking.

Creole Pumpkin Soup

FOO FOO (POUNDED PLANTAIN)

This recipe has its origins in Africa, and a Caribbean soup would not be complete without some of these. In Guyana we always made some type of soup on Sundays and my job was to pound the Foo Foo. I remember having to do battle with the plantains because they kept jumping out of the mortar each time I tried hitting them with the pestle. The pestle was over five feet tall and at the time I was only about 10 or 11 years old so it towered above me.

Fortunately, these days we have food processors to do the job.

In St Lucia this recipe is also served as a side dish to accompany Beef Stew and Stew Peas. The Foo Foo is placed in a greased teacup or small bowl to set the shape and then it is emptied on to the dinner plate.

INGREDIENTS
6 green plantains
1 tsp salt
water

Serves 6

METHOD
Peel plantains and place them in a saucepan with the salt and enough water to cover. Bring to the boil and simmer for about 25 minutes, or until the plantains are tender.

Next, place the plantains in a mortar and pound with the pestle. Dip the pestle in cold water to prevent sticking, and mash the plantains until smooth. Shape the mixture into golf balls and drop into the soup just before serving.

(See photo, page 41)

DHAL

The East Indian influence is very evident in this recipe. Curry powder and cumin give the yellow split peas new life!

INGREDIENTS

1 cup yellow split peas

1 onion *sliced*

2 cloves garlic *minced*

½ tsp roasted cumin *ground*

½ tsp curry powder

6 cups water

¼ Scotch bonnet *or* habanero
    pepper

3 cloves garlic *sliced*

¼ tsp cumin seeds

2 tbs vegetable oil

Serves 4

METHOD

Place all of the ingredients except the sliced garlic, oil and cumin seeds into a saucepan. Bring to the boil, reduce heat and simmer for 30 minutes. Purée with a hand blender.

Place the oil, garlic and cumin seeds in a ladle. Heat on an open flame until the garlic turns brown – about 2 minutes. Submerge the ladle into the saucepan.

Note:

It is very IMPORTANT that you cover the saucepan as soon as the oil hits the liquid.

EDDO SOUP

The African slaves in many of the islands were given small plots of land to cultivate crops, in an attempt to feed themselves. Root crops were very popular and this recipe is one that goes back to that time in our history.

INGREDIENTS

3 oz salt pork *diced*

1 large onion *sliced*

3 cloves garlic *minced*

1½ lb eddoes (tarro root) *peeled and diced*

1 tsp seasoned salt

2 green onions *chopped*

¼ tsp Scotch bonnet or habanero pepper *minced*

10 cups water

½ oz fresh thyme

½ oz fresh marjoram

½ oz fresh basil

3 tbs butter

½ oz parsley *minced*

Serves 6

METHOD

In a saucepan, brown the salt pork, then sauté the onion and garlic in the dripping for 3 minutes. Add the water, seasoned salt, eddoes, green onions and pepper. Tie the thyme, basil and marjoram together and lower into the pot. Bring to the boil and simmer for 30 minutes or until the eddoes are tender.

Discard the herbs, then purée the soup with a hand blender. Adjust seasonings to taste.

Stir in the butter and parsley, heat through and serve.

FISH AND COCONUT SOUP

The coconut milk in this recipe sets it apart from Fish Head Soup (which immediately follows). This dish has its origins in Curacao.

INGREDIENTS

3 lb fish fillets

1 large onion *sliced*

4 cloves garlic *minced*

2 bay leaves

¼ Scotch bonnet pepper

1 tsp cumin seeds

½ tsp thyme

½ tsp basil

4 oz salt pork *diced*

4 whole cloves

1 can (16 oz) coconut milk

8 cups water

2 carrots *sliced*

1 tsp seasoned salt

3 celery stalks *sliced*

4 tbs cornmeal

Serves 6

METHOD

In a stockpot, place the onion, garlic, salt pork, thyme, basil, water, coconut milk, bay leaves, cloves, cumin and hot pepper. Bring to the boil then reduce heat and simmer for 30 minutes.

Cut the fish into 1 inch cubes and add to the pot together with the celery, carrots and seasoned salt. Continue to simmer for 40 minutes. Adjust seasonings to taste.

Sprinkle on the cornmeal, stirring continuously. Cook for 2 more minutes.

FISH HEAD SOUP

Most of the islands have strong fishing communities and this recipe is served as a staple in many homes. Its popularity with the men folk can be directly linked to the soup's ability to put 'lead in your pencil'…

INGREDIENTS

2 large fish heads (approximately 2 pounds)

2 fresh limes

¼ cup butter *or* margarine

2 tomatoes *chopped*

1 onion *sliced*

6 cloves garlic *minced*

1 oz fresh thyme

1 oz fresh marjoram

1 tbs hot pepper sauce

¼ cup lemon juice

10 cups water

1 tbs seasoned salt

1 cup sliced celery

1 cup diced potatoes

salt *to taste*

Serves 6

METHOD

Clean fish heads and chop into chunks with a cleaver. Squeeze the juice of the limes on to the heads and rub with salt. Leave to stand for 10 minutes, then rinse and season with seasoned salt.

Melt the butter in a stockpot and sauté the onion, tomatoes and garlic for about 5 minutes. Add the fish heads and continue to cook for a further 5 minutes.

Pour in the water, pepper sauce, lemon juice, celery and seasoned salt together with the thyme and marjoram tied together.

Bring to the boil, reduce heat and simmer for 20 minutes. Add the potatoes and continue to simmer for a further 20 minutes. Adjust seasonings to your taste.

GROUNDNUT SOUP (PEANUT)

The Africans called peanuts groundnuts and that's how they are referred to even to this day.

In the countryside villages groundnuts are grown in kitchen gardens and sold by the housewives that tend the plots.

They reach the market fresh out of the ground with the mud still clinging to the pods. The nut on the inside is plump and juicy and tastes different from the commercial variety that has been roasted and salted.

This recipe is from the island of St Kitts.

INGREDIENTS

4 tbs vegetable oil

1 large onion *chopped*

2 cups smooth peanut butter

1½ cups evaporated milk

7 cups water

¼ Scotch bonnet *or* habanero
     pepper *minced*

1 cup dry sherry

5 dashes Angostura Bitters

Serves 6

METHOD

Sauté the onion in the oil until limp, then stir in the peanut butter. Continue to stir for about 2 minutes, or until the peanut butter starts to melt. Pour in the milk and mix well, then the water. Add the hot pepper, bitters and sherry.

Simmer for 30 minutes, stirring frequently.

JAMAICAN RED PEAS SOUP

This is another perfect example of a soup being a complete meal. Jamaicans have an on-going love affair with red kidney beans and they can be found in many of their traditional dishes.

INGREDIENTS

1 lb red kidney beans *soaked overnight, or* 4 cups canned variety

1 lb beef *cut into cubes*

8 oz salt pork *cubed*

1 onion *sliced*

2 green onions *chopped*

1 oz fresh thyme

1oz fresh marjoram

1 tbs hot pepper sauce

seasoned salt *to taste*

1 lb yams *peeled and cut into thick slices*

1 lb sweet potatoes *peeled and cut into thick slices*

14 cups water

1 tsp ground allspice

Dumplings

12 oz flour / 2 cups flour

½ tsp salt

water *to mix dumplings*

Serves 8

METHOD

Tie the marjoram and thyme together, then place in a large stockpot together with all the other ingredients. Bring to the boil, reduce heat and simmer until the beef and peas are tender. Now make the dumplings and put them into the soup when the beef and peas are tender.

Make the dumplings by mixing the flour, salt and water together to make a stiff consistency. Knead on a floured board for 5 minutes, then shape into small round balls (or roll them into pieces the length of your little finger) and drop into the soup.

Continue to cook for a further 15 minutes.

(See **Note** on page 33 re cooking peas/beans.)

MANNISH WATER

This Jamaican soup is made from ramgoat offal and other disposables.

Traditionally Mannish Water was cooked outdoors on a wood fire in a large tin that originally contained vegetable oil. It is said to 'put lead in your pencil' and therefore has a very large following. It is sold at street corners, in gas stations, in rumshops and the like. Served in a disposable hot cup, the patron drinks the liquid then eats the rest with a fork.

Goat Water is the name given to this speciality in St Vincent. When a group of fellas gets together for a 'beach cook' this is what they are likely to serve up. I wonder if its reported aphrodisiac qualities has anything to do with this? The Vincentian version of this recipe uses pieces of goat meat and coconut dumplings.

INGREDIENTS

3 lb ramgoat disposables – head,
    feet, liver, etc

7 green bananas

2 medium carrots

2 lb yam

2 lb dasheen (tarro)

2 oz fresh thyme

1 large onion *diced*

3 cloves garlic *minced*

3 green onions *chopped*

1 tbs hot pepper sauce

seasoned salt *to taste*

¼ cup margarine

1 tsp black pepper

1 tsp ground allspice

Dumplings

2 cups flour

½ tsp salt

water *to mix dumplings*

Coconut Dumplings

To the above ingredients add: ½ cup
    grated or desicated coconut

METHOD

Wash and cut the meat into chunks, then season with salt, thyme, onion, garlic, green onions and pepper sauce. Place in a covered bowl and leave to marinate for 2 hours.

In a large stockpot place the meat and 8 pints water, pepper, allspice, margarine and salt to taste. Bring to the boil, reduce heat and simmer for 1 hour.

In the meantime, wash the green bananas and cut off the tops and tails. Slice into 1 inch rounds (do not peel).

Peel and dice the carrots, dasheen and yam and set aside.

To make the dumplings, mix the flour, salt and coconut together. Add enough water to make a stiff consistency and knead for 2 minutes on a floured board. Break the dough into tiny pieces and roll them into the shape of your little finger.

After the meat has simmered for an hour, add the green bananas, dasheen, carrots, yams and dumplings and continue to cook for 30 minutes. Adjust seasonings to your taste.

Note:

This can also be prepared using fish instead of meat. The fish should be sprinkled with salt and lime juice; then rinsed after 10 minutes. At this point it is ready to be boiled with the salt, garlic, onions, thyme, green onions and pepper sauce for 10 minutes.

Add the remaining ingredients as per the above recipe.

The folks in St Vincent call this one 'Boilene'.

THE CAYMAN ISLANDS

At the time that they were sighted by Christopher Columbus in 1503, the Cayman Islands were home to large numbers of crocodiles and turtles – as a matter of fact 'Cayman' is derived from 'Caiman' a Carib word for the type of crocodile which lived there.

As might be expected, in a relatively short time both the turtles and the crocodiles were hunted to extinction although today, thanks mainly to a turtle-farming project, turtles once more can be seen in the surrounding waters.

For a long time the only people interested in the islands were the hunters and the pirates who could always recognise a good piece of real-estate when they saw it. Today, the historical links to the pirates are celebrated during Pirates Week which is held every year between the last week of October and the first week of November.

Things started to change after 1670 when the island was recognised as part of Jamaica. It was then colonised from Jamaica and played an important role as a port of call for sailing ships during that era.

Today the Cayman Islands are among the wealthiest islands in the Caribbean with a vibrant tourism and banking industry.

Interesting facts about the Cayman Islands

- The Cayman Islands is the fifth largest financial centre in the world and home to more than 500 banks.
- Many visitors to Grand Cayman get the chance to pay a visit to 'Hell'. The area, with its eerie coral and limestone formations, is located at the North Western tip of the island and was given this name by one of the island's commissioners because of its desolate appearance. The highlight of a visit to this area is to mail postcards – the postmark reads *'Hell, Grand Cayman'*!

RED CONCH CHOWDER

In the Cayman Islands, this is one of their specialities. It differs from the usual way of making a chowder because the base is tomato. I hope you enjoy this variation.

INGREDIENTS

2 lb fresh conch

4 tbs fresh lime juice

2 tsp salt

2 onions *chopped*

3 stalks celery *diced*

1 tbs tomato paste

seasoned salt *to taste*

2 green onions *chopped*

⅛ tsp Scotch bonnet *or* habanero pepper *minced*

4 potatoes *peeled and diced*

1 can (16 oz) stewed tomatoes

1 can (16 oz) red kidney beans

1 oz fresh thyme

1 oz fresh marjoram

1 oz fresh basil

4 tbs butter

6 pints water

Serves 6

METHOD

Wash and clean the conch then pound it with a meat tenderiser or hammer until in becomes flattened and is between ½ – ¼ inch thick. Rub it with the lime juice and salt and allow it to stand for 15 minutes.

Rinse the conch and boil in salted water for 15 minutes. Coarsely chop it in a food processor and set aside.

Heat the butter in a stockpot and sauté the onion and green onions for 3 minutes, then add the celery and cook for a further 2 minutes. Pour in the water and add the tomato paste, pepper, seasoned salt, potatoes, kidney beans and stewed tomatoes. Tie the herbs together and drop them into the pot. Bring to the boil and simmer for 30 minutes. Add the conch and simmer for 20 minutes more.

Serve with garlic croutons and parmesan cheese.

Red Conch Chowder

OKRA SLUSH

A Barbadian favourite, this dish is referred to locally as a stew. It looks similar to Gumbo from New Orleans.

INGREDIENTS

1 lb okras
2 tomatoes *chopped*
1 onion *diced*
4 cloves garlic *minced*
1 tsp hot pepper sauce
½ tsp thyme
½ tsp basil
½ tsp marjoram
2 oz salt pork
7 cups water

Serves 4

METHOD

Wash okras and remove head and tails. Cut into ½ inch cartwheels.

Place all of the ingredients in a stockpot and bring to the boil. Reduce heat and simmer for 30 minutes. After this the okras should have disintegrated and the liquid reduced to three quarters.

Adjust seasonings to your taste.

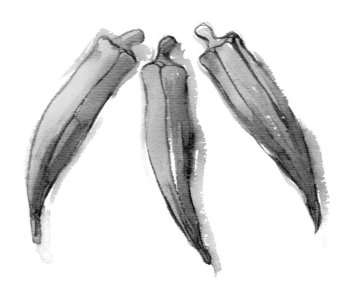

SPLIT PEAS AND PUMPKIN SOUP

*We refer to this one in the Caribbean as 'Restaurant Food'.
Traditionally, soups are a complete meal. This one, however, is not
and can be found on the menus of many restaurants.*

INGREDIENTS

1 cup dried split peas *washed and
    soaked in water for 2 hours*

3 cups pumpkin *diced*

2 cups potatoes *diced*

1 onion *chopped*

4 cloves garlic *minced*

½ tsp basil

½ oregano

½ thyme

1 tsp seasoned salt

8 cups water

6 oz ham *diced*

1 cup evaporated milk

Serves 6

METHOD

Drain the split peas, then place all of the ingredients except the
milk into a saucepan and boil until tender (approximately 1 hour).
Purée with a hand blender. Add the milk and heat through.

VIRGIN ISLANDS
RED PEAS SOUP

This next recipe is from the Virgin Islands and is the perfect example of a 'one-pot' dish. In the old days it was the main meal of the day and could be served as often as twice in any given week. Although similar to the Jamaican version, the difference was marked enough for me to share both with you.

INGREDIENTS

1½ cups red kidney beans *soaked overnight, or* 3 cups canned variety

8 oz salt pork *cubed*

3 inch piece of orange peel

1 tsp fresh ginger *minced*

4 carrots *sliced*

2 large onions *chopped*

1 tsp fresh parsley

1 tsp fresh, chopped celery

¼ tsp marjoram

¼ tsp thyme

10 cups water

1 ripe plantain

1 large tomato *chopped*

6 cloves garlic *minced*

2 green onions *chopped*

1 lb sweet potatoes

½ lb pumpkin *diced*

1½ cups sugar

seasoned salt *to taste*

Serves 8

METHOD

Wash and drain the peas then place them in a stockpot with the water, ginger, orange peel and salt pork. Bring to the boil and simmer until the peas are tender.

Add the remaining ingredients, and continue to simmer for a further 45 minutes.

In the meantime make the dumplings (see page 4), and add them to the soup 15 minutes before the end.

(See **Note** on page 33 re cooking peas/beans.)

Virgin Islands Red Peas Soup

CUTTERS AND THE LIKE

A 'cutter' in Barbados is some kind of meat, fish, cheese, or even a vegetable like avocado, in a loaf of bread. That may seem simple enough – until we define what is meant by 'loaf'. A loaf of bread or a plain old salt bread is a little bigger than a hamburger bun with a bit more crust, is a lot heavier in texture, and has a very distinctive taste.

When you combine this loaf with something like ham or cheese it becomes a cutter – not to be confused with a sandwich, which is made from two slices of square sandwich bread which are usually buttered before anything else is done, and which is just not as interesting. For one thing the ham in a ham cutter is always sugar-cured picnic ham which is taken from the oven to the serving counter, while the ham in a ham sandwich is deli-style ham.

Now, a ham cutter is ham in salt bread, while a cheese cutter is cheese in salt bread, put the two together in the same loaf and your cutter becomes a 'Dagwood' while two fish cakes in salt bread become 'Bread 'n Two'. Combine cheese and fish cakes in the same loaf and the cutter becomes a 'Cheese 'n One' or a 'Cheese 'n Two' (the 'one' or 'two' referring to the number of fish cakes).

Cutters are always served with an accompanying bottle of pepper sauce in the same way as you would expect ketchup with fries.

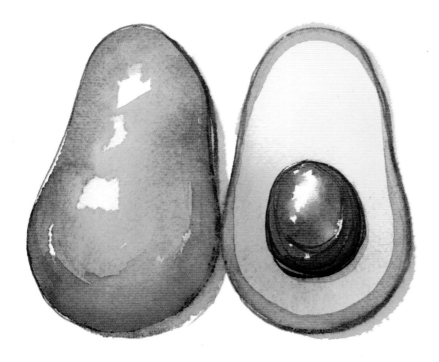

1 2 3

This is what I call 'Hurry-up Food'. It takes very little time to prepare and also tastes quite good. The name represents the three main ingredients. Pasta is well represented in the diets of many Caribbean people.

INGREDIENTS

4 potatoes *peeled and quartered*

1 pack (12 oz) macaroni elbows

1 can (12 oz) corned beef

2 tbs Barbadian Seasoning (see recipe page 123)

¼ tsp seasoned salt

1 tbs tomato paste

1 tbs vegetable oil

¼ cup water

Serves 4

METHOD

Cook the macaroni and potatoes in salted water, drain and set aside.

Sauté the Barbadian Seasoning in the oil for 1 minute then add the corned beef.

Stir in the tomato paste, seasoned salt and water, cover and simmer for 3 minutes.

Stir in the macaroni and potatoes and heat through.

BARBADIAN RICE AND STEW

In Barbados, a restaurant menu would not be complete without this cornerstone of Barbadian cuisine. From the most humble home to the grand mansions, this dish crosses all boundaries.

INGREDIENTS

1 lb stew beef

1 tbs gravy browning

2 tbs tomato ketchup

1 cup water

2 tbs vegetable oil

1 large carrot *peeled and sliced*

2 medium potatoes *peeled and quartered*

2 tbs Barbadian Seasoning (see recipe page 123)

¼ tsp seasoned salt

2 cups long grain rice *soaked in water for 2 hours*

½ cup pigeon peas *soaked in water overnight, or* 1 cup canned variety.

1 oz salt pork

½ tsp thyme

4 cups water

Serves 4

METHOD

Wash and cut the beef into bite-sized pieces, then rub with the Barbadian Seasoning and tomato ketchup.

Heat the oil in a skillet and stir-fry the meat for 10 minutes.

Pour in the gravy browning and cook for a further 5 minutes. Add the water, cover and simmer for 30 minutes.

Stir in the carrot and potatoes, adjust the seasonings with a little seasoned salt, and cook for another 15 minutes. Add a little more water if necessary.

Cook until the meat is tender – usually about 45 minutes to 1 hour total cooking time.

For the rice. . .

Place the peas, salt pork and the thyme in a pan with 4 cups water and bring to the boil. Reduce heat and simmer for 30 minutes, or until the peas are tender.

Wash and drain the rice and add to the pan. Pour in enough water to just be level with the rice and peas mixture. Bring to the boil then reduce heat to its lowest level, cover and simmer for about 20 minutes or until all the water has evaporated.

(See **Note** on page 33 re cooking peas/beans.)

Note:

Rice that has been soaked does not require a lot of liquid to cook; also the cooking time is reduced.

BEEF *OR* CHICKEN PELAU

This is a great one for keeping the hunger pangs at bay for a long time. When Caribbean people go to a party there is always a lot of drinking involved. It is therefore necessary to have a 'solid foundation' to rally the night.

Rice, being one of the main stays in the Caribbean diet, is the preferred 'foundation' at such events in places like Trinidad, Guyana, the Virgin Islands and St Vincent.

INGREDIENTS

1 large chicken *cut into 10–12 pieces, or* 2 lb stew beef *cut into cubes*

3 tbs Barbadian Seasoning (see recipe page 123)

3 salted, cured pig-tails *soaked in hot water for at least 4 hours*

3 seasoning peppers *cut in half* (optional)

seasoned salt *to taste*

4 tbs vegetable oil

½ cup brown sugar

1 can (16 oz) pigeon peas *drained*

2½ cups long grain rice *washed then soaked in water for 2 hours*

1 tbs hot pepper sauce

½ tsp mixed herbs (thyme, oregano, marjoram)

3 tsp cilantro (coriander) *minced*

Serves 6

METHOD

Season the chicken or beef with Barbadian Seasoning and set aside.

Heat the oil in a pan, then add brown sugar stirring until it starts to caramelise. Add the chicken or beef and 'brown down' stirring constantly for about 10 minutes.

Drain the pig-tails, chop them in half and add to the pot along with the seasoning peppers. Continue to stir for another 5 minutes then pour over 3 cups water and cover. Simmer for 30 minutes, or until the meat is tender.

Stir in the pigeon peas, mixed herbs, cilantro, pepper sauce and drained rice with enough water to just about cover the mixture. Adjust seasonings to taste, for example, a bit more sugar is often needed.

Bring to the boil then reduce heat to lowest level, cover and cook for 20–30 minutes or until all of the liquid has evaporated.

CABBAGE AND CORNED BEEF

For the cook 'on the run', this recipe from Martinique is fast, easy and – best of all – very tasty.

INGREDIENTS

1 can (12 oz) corned beef

3 cups cabbage *cut up in chunks*

1 onion *diced*

4 cloves garlic *minced*

1 tsp hot pepper sauce

¼ tsp seasoned salt

2 tbs tomato paste

1 tsp mixed herbs (thyme, oregano, marjoram)

2 cups water

2 tbs vegetable oil

Serves 4

METHOD

Heat the oil in a pan and sauté the onion and garlic for 2 minutes. Add the corned beef, cabbage, tomato paste, pepper sauce, seasoned salt, herbs and water. Simmer for 20 minutes or until the cabbage is tender. Add water if necessary and stir frequently.

Serve over boiled rice or pasta.

CARIBBEAN MEAT SAUCE WITH SPAGHETTI

Cooks in the Caribbean have taken this Italian dish one step further… With a shake of this and a dash of that, the 'Caribbeanising' is now complete!

INGREDIENTS

6 oz minced meat

1 can (16 oz) tomato sauce

1 tbs tomato paste

1 onion

6 cloves garlic

½ tsp dried basil

½ tsp dried marjoram

½ tsp dried oregano

½ tsp dried thyme

½ tsp hot pepper sauce

½ tsp salt

1 oz cheddar cheese *cut into cubes*

2 cups water

1 pack (12 oz) spaghetti *prepared according to package directions*

Serves 4

METHOD

Place all of the ingredients except the minced meat into a blender and purée for 1 minute. Pour into a stockpot and simmer for 40 minutes. Add the minced meat, adjust the seasonings to taste, and simmer for a further 20 minutes.

Serve over hot spaghetti.

Caribbean Meat Sauce with Spaghetti

CARIBBEAN SHEPHERD'S PIE

Breadfruit is ideal for this dish. Its slightly sweet flavour complements the other ingredients.

The breadfruit tree was brought to the Caribbean by Captain William Bligh from Tahiti. His first attempt to introduce the tree to the Caribbean failed in April 1789. This story is told in the film Mutiny On The Bounty. *In 1793 he was successful in his mission and now the tree grows profusely in every island and many people either know someone or are related to someone that has a tree growing in their backyard. Of course, this means that in the season the average household will be served breadfruit on a regular basis in many different ways.*

INGREDIENTS

1 breadfruit *or* 3 lb yams *peeled and boiled in salted water then mashed*

12 oz minced meat

1 onion *minced*

6 cloves garlic *minced*

½ tsp seasoned salt

1 tbs hot pepper sauce

1 tsp mixed herbs (thyme, oregano, marjoram)

1 tbs tomato paste

2 tbs breadcrumbs

2 tbs vegetable oil

1 can (16 oz) mixed vegetables

½ cup water

Serves 6

METHOD

Add a little butter and milk to the mashed breadfruit or yam to make a smooth consistency. Set aside.

Sauté the onion and garlic in the oil for 2 minutes, then add the minced meat.

Season with the pepper sauce, seasoned salt, tomato paste and herbs and continue to cook for a few minutes. Pour in ½ cup water, cover and simmer for 5 minutes.

Add breadcrumbs to absorb any excess liquid, then stir in mixed vegetables and turn off heat.

Grease an oven-proof dish and line it with half the mashed breadfruit or yam. Pour in the minced meat and top with the remainder of the mashed yam or breadfruit.

Brush with melted butter and bake in a preheated oven at 350 °F degree for 30 minutes.

GROS ISLET

This sleepy little seaside village located on the North coast of St Lucia, goes through a metamorphosis every Friday night. The main street is blocked off, and 'sky-high' speakers are erected. All the shops open their doors to the visitors and locals who are sure to come to Gros Islet for the action. Tables and chairs are placed in the street. Everywhere you go the smell of barbecued chicken or lambi (conch) goes with you as the several vendors compete with each other and with the shops in selling food and liquor. The lambi features prominently here, barbecued on skewers and served hot off the grill with a spicy sauce.

The music begins to play, and even your bones vibrate to the pounding bass. All around you people are having a good time, dancing, drinking and eating. The fête lasts until sun-up when the last party animals finally decide they have had enough and crawl back to their hotels.

Shortly afterwards the street cleaners come out and, within hours, the streets are spotlessly clean again as the village once more returns to its sleepy state … until the next Friday night.

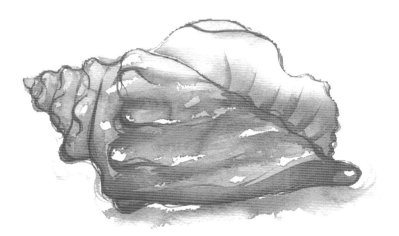

CHANNA AND BEEF STEW

The garbanzo bean or chick pea is called 'channa' in the Caribbean and is used in a variety of recipes. This recipe comes from Guyana.

INGREDIENTS

1 lb stew beef

½ cup channa (garbanzos) *soaked in water overnight, or* 1 cup canned variety

1 onion *chopped*

4 cloves garlic *minced*

½ tsp seasoned salt

1 tsp hot pepper sauce

2 tbs tomato ketchup

1 tsp mixed herbs (thyme, oregano, marjoram)

2 tbs tomato paste

2 tbs vegetable oil

2 cups water

Serves 4

METHOD

Boil the garbanzos in salted water until tender, drain and set aside.

Wash and cut the meat into bite-sized pieces. Season with onion, garlic, herbs, seasoned salt, pepper sauce and tomato ketchup.

Heat the oil in a pan and stir-fry the meat for about 10 minutes. Pour in the water and tomato paste, cover and simmer for 30 minutes. Add more water if necessary.

Add the garbanzos, adjust seasonings to taste and simmer for a further 15 minutes. The meat should be tender but, if not, continue to cook a while longer.

Serve over boiled rice or pasta.

(See **Note** on page 33 re cooking peas/beans.)

Channa and Beef Stew with rice

COOK-UP RICE

On New Year's Eve, many people go out to parties that last until six o'clock the next morning. However, there are some folks who prefer to ring in the new year in a more peaceful manner. This next recipe is the traditional dish that is served at such gatherings in Guyana.

INGREDIENTS

1½ lb beef *cut into bite-sized pieces*

¾ cup blackeye peas *soaked in water overnight, or* 1 can (16 oz) canned variety

3 oz salt pork

2 tbs tomato ketchup

1 tsp mixed herbs (thyme, marjoram, basil)

1 small onion *chopped*

5 cloves garlic *minced*

1 cup coconut milk

2 tsp seasoned salt

1 tbs hot pepper sauce

3 cups long grain rice *soaked in water for 2 hours*

3 tbs vegetable oil

Beef Tripe

4 oz tripe

juice of 1 lime

salt *to taste*

1 pint water

Serves 6

METHOD

Season the beef with half the herbs, half the seasoned salt, the tomato ketchup, pepper sauce, onion and garlic.

Heat the oil in a saucepan and sauté the beef for 5 minutes. Add the blackeye peas, that have been washed and drained, then the salt pork and continue to cook for 3 minutes. Pour in the coconut milk with 4 cups water and bring to the boil. Reduce heat, and simmer for 30–40 minutes, or until the beef and peas are tender.

Add the washed and drained rice with enough water to cover. Stir in the remaining herbs and seasoned salt and bring to a full boil. Adjust the seasoning to your taste then reduce heat to lowest level, cover and cook until all the liquid has evaporated and the rice is tender. This should take approximately 25 minutes.

Beef Tripe (Optional)
In the Caribbean we use Beef Tripe in this dish together with the cubed beef.
Clean the tripe and soak in lime juice and salt for about 10 minutes.

Wash thoroughly and cut into ½ inch strips. Season the same way as the beef, and stir-fry for a few minutes in a pressure cooker. Add 1 pint of water and pressure-cook for 20 minutes.

The tripe can now be added to the main saucepan.

Adjust the seasonings to your taste.

Note:
The peas/beans can take a while to become tender so, if possible, cook them separately in a pressure cooker for 35 minutes.

JAMAICAN STEW PEAS
WITH BEEF

As mentioned before, Jamaicans love red kidney beans and this stew is one of their favourites. Coconut milk always enhances any dish to which it is added.

INGREDIENTS

2 cups red kidney beans (peas)
　soaked overnight, or 2 cans (16
　oz) canned variety
½ lb salt pork
1 onion *chopped*
5 cloves garlic *minced*
1 lb beef *cubed*
2 tbs ketchup
1 tbs mixed herbs (thyme, basil,
　marjoram, etc)
seasoned salt *to taste*
1 tsp hot pepper sauce
2 cups water
2 cups coconut milk
2 tbs butter
2 tbs vegetable oil
1 tsp ground allspice

Dumplings
2 cups flour
½ tsp salt

Serves 4

METHOD

Soak the salt pork in hot water for about 1 hour then drain and cut up into small pieces.

In the meantime, season the beef with the onion, garlic, seasoned salt, pepper sauce, ketchup and herbs and allspice.

Heat the oil in a pan and sauté the beef for 10 minutes. Then add the red peas, salt pork, water and coconut milk. Bring to the boil, reduce the heat and simmer until the beef and peas are tender.

When the peas and beef are cooked, make the dumplings. Add a little water to the flour and salt. Knead the dough for 2 minutes then form tiny dumplings about the shape and size of your little finger. Add them to the stew.

Adjust seasonings to taste and continue cooking for 15 minutes. Just before removing from the heat stir in the butter.

Serve over boiled rice.

(See **Note** on page 33 re cooking peas/beans.)

JAMAICAN BEEF PATTIES

Wherever there is a Jamaican community in the US, Canada or England these patties are found being manufactured commercially. However, if you are not fortunate enough to live close to one of them, here's your chance to bring a taste of Jamaica home.

INGREDIENTS

Pastry

1 tsp salt

½ cup iced water *mixed with a few drops yellow food colouring*

1½ lb shortening

4 cups flour

Filling

2 lb minced beef

8 cloves garlic *minced*

2 tsp mixed herbs, (thyme, basil, marjoram, etc.)

1 tsp seasoned salt

2 green onions *finely chopped*

1 tbs hot pepper sauce

4 oz bread

½ tsp MSG (optional)

3 tbs tomato ketchup

4 tbs vegetable oil

Serves 8

METHOD

First, mix the pastry by mixing the flour and salt, then cut in the shortening. Add enough iced water to enable the dough to be rolled out.

Pat the dough with a rolling pin and turn a couple of times to ensure that the dough holds together. Wrap in tin foil and place in the freezer until ready for use.

Second, mix the meat, the green onions, seasoned salt, garlic, pepper sauce and half of the herbs. Heat the oil in a pan and stir-fry this mixture for about 10 minutes over a low flame.

Pour off any excess oil. Now cover the bread with water and leave it to soak for a few minutes. When it is thoroughly soaked, break it up with a spoon, add the remainder of the herbs and cook over a low flame until the bread is dry.

Add the meat to the bread mixture, adjust seasonings to taste, then add the ketchup and MSG, and cook for a further 15 minutes. Cool before putting in the pastry.

Third, roll the pastry to ⅛ inch thick then cut into 4 inch circles. Place 3 tablespoons of the filling in the middle of each circle, wet the bottom edge of the circle with water then fold and seal with the edge of a fork.

Finally, place the patties on a greased cookie sheet and bake in a preheated oven at 350 °F for 20 minutes.

Note:
This is traditionally a very hot and spicy patty.

OKRAS AND BEEF STEW

Okras are very popular in Guyana and this dish is a typical example of how to make a small quantity of meat go a long way. Depending on the fortunes of the family, another ½ lb okras could be added to stretch the meat even further.

INGREDIENTS

1 lb beef *cut into bite-sized pieces*

1 large onion *minced*

4 garlic cloves *minced*

seasoned salt *to taste*

1 tsp hot pepper sauce

1 tsp thyme

1 tsp marjoram

2 tbs vegetable oil

12 oz okras *cleaned with heads and
    tails removed*

4 tomatoes *chopped*

1 cup coconut milk

Serves 4

METHOD

Season the meat with the onion, garlic, thyme, marjoram, seasoned salt and pepper sauce.

Heat the oil in a saucepan and sauté the meat for 10 minutes, stirring frequently. Add the okras and tomatoes and continue cooking for 5 minutes.

Pour over the coconut milk, adjust seasonings to taste and simmer for 20 minutes, or until the beef is tender.

Serve with boiled rice.

Okras and Beef Stew, garnished with baby carrots, okra slices and red pepper

OKRAS COOK-UP RICE

This is the Guyanese version of this popular rice dish. In some islands it is done with salted cod instead of beef.

INGREDIENTS

1 lb stew beef *cut up into ¾ inch pieces*

2 tbs tomato ketchup

3 tbs Barbadian Seasoning (see recipe on page 123)

2 tbs vegetable oil

3 salted pig-tails *soaked in hot water and left to stand for four hours*

1 tsp basil

1 tsp marjoram

½ tsp MSG (optional)

1½ cups coconut milk

8 oz okras *cut into cartwheels*

3 seasoning peppers* *cut in half* (optional)

3 cups long grain rice *washed and soaked in water for 2 hours*

seasoning salt *to taste*

3 cups water

Serves 6

METHOD

Season the beef with Barbadian Seasoning and ketchup.

Heat the oil in a saucepan and stir-fry the beef for 5 minutes.

Drain and cut the pig-tails in half and add to the pot. Continue to stir-fry for a further 5 minutes.

Next, add three cups of water, the coconut milk, herbs, seasoning peppers and simmer for 30 minutes or until the beef is tender.

Add the okras and continue to boil for a further 5 minutes.

Drain the rice and add to the contents of the pot; stir, then add enough water to just cover the mixture.

Adjust the seasonings, for example add seasoning salt and a little more Barbadian Seasoning, herbs and MSG. Bring to the boil, then reduce the heat to the lowest level, cover and simmer for 25 minutes or until all the liquid is absorbed.

Note:

*Seasoning pepper: a variety of pepper that has very little heat but a strong aroma and flavour.

Okras Cook-up Rice and Tropical Coleslaw, garnished with a few pieces of pig's tail

ARAWAKS AND PEPPERPOT

Caribbean history began long before the arrival of Columbus. As a matter of fact, the Caribbean itself takes its name from the fierce Caribs, a race of cannibals who terrorised the other inhabitants of the islands at that time – the peaceful Arawaks. In the following pages we will be telling you about the contributions of the original Caribbean inhabitants to our culture, particularly in relation to cooking.

All the peaceful Arawaks ever wanted to do was to be left alone to grow their corn and manioc, to fish and to catch the occasional agouti. Since they weren't very good hunters, their main food source was manioc, which just happened to be a very poisonous root. The Arawaks had long since learned how to extract the poison from the root. This was done with the aid of a woven *matapi* and a few children. The *matapi,* which was woven from palms and vines, was about ten feet long and resembled a snake; it was filled with grated manioc and hung from a tall tree. At the other end it was fitted with a hoop through which a piece of wood was passed. Children took turns sitting on this end. The weight of the children resulted in the *matapi* being stretched and the juice was thus squeezed from the grated manioc and collected in a container placed underneath.

The poisonous liquid was discarded and the resulting cassava flour made into cassava bread (more of a biscuit than bread) which was one of the mainstays of the Arawak diet.

As time progressed, the Arawaks realised that if the liquid was left in the sun, it lost its poison and turned to a dark brown colour. They found this made an excellent natural preservative and was given the name 'casareep'. This magical liquid is still used today and forms the basis of my next recipe: Pepperpot.

The great thing about Pepperpot is that all you need to do with it is to keep adding meat and boiling the liquid at least once per day to maintain its preservative qualities. Thus, the Arawaks could put their fish or vegetables into the pot and boil it and keep going on forever.

In the Caribbean today we normally keep Pepperpot going for several weeks at a time – although it does not always form the main course but is often used as a side dish.

So what else did the Arawaks do? Well, they kept running for their lives, not only from the fierce Caribs who used them as a major food source, but from people like Columbus and his cronies, who slaughtered them without mercy.

In the midst of this they developed jewellery from shells and stones and were probably the original soccer stars of the world. They played a game on a field similar in dimensions to a present-day soccer or rugby field. The game was played with a rubber ball and was found to be almost identical to one played by the Maya in Mexico. Since rubber was not present in the Caribbean, it is assumed that the ball and the game probably originated in Mexico.

Unlike their male counterparts, some of the Arawak women escaped being eaten by the Caribs. They were used as breeders by the Caribs and it is debatable as to who met with a worse fate since the Caribs were not exactly the gentlemen of the Century.

PEPPERPOT

Pepperpot, Garlic Pork and Green Plantain Chips

This Arawak speciality was used as a meat preserver. On their return from the hunt, the Arawak men would put their catch in a big pot which contained the leftovers from previous days. The primary ingredient of the pot was casareep which was made from the juice of the bitter cassava root. The casareep acted as a natural preservative and the meat in the pot lasted for several months without refrigeration as long as it was brought to the boil for a few minutes each day and only clean spoons used when stirring or serving.

The secrets of the Arawaks are still practised today in the preparation of this famous dish. It should be made at least three to four days before serving since the true flavour does not develop immediately.

INGREDIENTS

½ lb stew beef (marbled with fat) *cut into 2 inch cubes*

2 lb cow heel / cow foot *cut into ¾ inch thick circles by the butcher*

1½ lb shoulder pork *cut into 2 inch cubes*

4 salted pig-tails *(soak in hot water and leave to stand for 4 hours)*

10 whole cloves

1 stick cinnamon (6 inches)

salt *to taste*

1 Scotch bonnet *or* habanero pepper *cut in half*

1½ cups casareep

¼ cup sugar

6 cups water

Serves 10

METHOD

First drain and cut the pig-tails in half. Next, place the cow heel in a pressure cooker together with the pig-tails, water, cloves, cinnamon, sugar, casareep and hot pepper. Pressure cook for 1 hour.

Allow to cool until the pressure dissipates, then open and add the pork, beef and salt. Add sufficient water to bring the liquid to 1½ inches below the level of the meat. Cover and pressure-cook for a further 30 minutes.

This dish is usually served with bread, boiled rice or Foo Foo.

Notes:

Leave to stand for three days before serving. Bring to the boil for 5 minutes each day.

The older the Pepperpot the better it tastes.

SPAGHETTI AND CORNED BEEF

This is a 'meal in a hurry'. It takes only about 30 minutes to prepare and tastes really good – not to mention it fills a hole. A Barbadian friend of mine introduced me to this one many years ago and it has become a favourite with my family.

INGREDIENTS

1 onion *minced*

4 cloves garlic *minced*

2 tbs vegetable oil

¼ tsp seasoned salt

¼ tsp mixed herbs (thyme, oregano, marjoram)

1 tbs tomato paste

½ tsp hot pepper sauce

¼ cup water

1 can (12 oz) corned beef

1 pack (12 oz) spaghetti

Serves 4

METHOD

Cook the spaghetti according to package instructions and set aside.

Heat the oil in a pan and sauté the onion and garlic for 3 minutes. Add the corned beef and continue to cook for 1 minute. Add the seasoned salt, mixed herbs, tomato paste, pepper sauce and water, stirring all the time. Cover and leave to simmer for 5 minutes on very low heat.

Mix in the spaghetti and turn off the heat when it is warm throughout.

ST LUCIAN BEEF STEW

This stew reflects its French heritage. The browning of the sugar is the secret to getting this done 'just right'. Use a heavy saucepan and stir the sugar continuously. When the caramel changes from a light to dark brown add the beef to the saucepan.

INGREDIENTS

1½ lb stew beef *cut into 1 inch cubes*

5 cloves garlic

1 medium onion *chopped*

seasoned salt *to taste*

1 tsp hot pepper sauce

⅛ tsp marjoram

⅛ tsp basil

1 oz fresh cilantro (coriander) *chopped*

1 oz green onions *chopped*

⅛ tsp ground cloves

¼ cup brown sugar

1 large tomato *chopped*

¼ cup vegetable oil

Serves 4

METHOD

Season the meat with the onion, garlic, cilantro, green onions, pepper sauce, herbs, cloves and seasoned salt, and set aside.

Heat the oil in a heavy saucepan, then pour in the sugar. Stir the sugar continuously. It will start to melt and become a light brown liquid. As it continues to cook it will change to a darker colour and look a little thicker. At this point add the beef and tomato. Stir-fry for 10 minutes.

Pour in 1 cup water, bring to the boil, reduce the heat and simmer for 10 minutes. Repeat this process until the meat is tender. Do not add more water until the previous set has almost evaporated. This stew does not have much gravy.

Serve with Breadfruit Salad, Stew Peas, Foo Foo and boiled rice.

St Lucian Beef Stew, Foo Foo, St Lucian Stew Peas and boiled rice

STUFFED PAPAYA

Stuffing vegetables and fruits with spicy minced meat is common to most of our islands.

You can try this recipe also with pumpkin, christophene or eggplant.

INGREDIENTS

2 small papayas *cut in half lengthwise* (the fruit can either be ripe or half ripe)

Stuffing

2 tbs vegetable oil
6 green onions *minced*
3 cloves garlic *minced*
12 oz lean minced beef
½ tsp hot pepper sauce
2 tomatoes *peeled and chopped*
2 tbs raisins
½ cup cashew nuts *chopped*
½ cup parmesan cheese
seasoned salt *to taste*

Serves 4

METHOD

Remove the seeds from the papayas and discard.

Next, make the stuffing. Heat the oil in a pan and sauté the green onions and garlic for 2 minutes. Add the minced beef, pepper sauce and seasoned salt and continue to cook for 8 minutes, until browned.

Add the tomatoes, raisins and cashews, cooking and stirring until all the liquid has evaporated (about 5 minutes). Remove from the heat and stir in 2 tablespoons cheese. Spoon the mixture into the papaya cavities and sprinkle with the remaining cheese.

Once stuffed, place the papayas in a shallow roasting pan and pour in enough boiling water to come quarter way up the fruit.

Bake in a preheated oven at 350 °F for 30 minutes.

chicken

BARBADIAN FRIED CHICKEN

Barbadians are one of the largest consumers of chicken (per capita) in the world. Of the many ways that it is prepared in Barbados, this is the most popular.

INGREDIENTS

4 chicken legs (drumstick and
     thigh)
4 tbs Barbadian Seasoning (see
     recipe page 123)
1 lime
1 tsp salt
2 tbs Worcestershire sauce
1 tsp granulated garlic
¼ tsp ground black pepper
2 cups all-purpose flour
2 tsp seasoned salt
1 tsp baking powder
2 eggs *beaten*
vegetable oil *for frying*

Serves 2

METHOD

Wash and clean the chicken removing any excess skin and fat. Squeeze juice from the lime on to the chicken and rub in the salt. Leave to stand for 5 minutes, then rinse and pat dry.

Cut slits in the meat close to the bone and force some of the Barbadian Seasoning in. Rub the rest together with the Worcestershire sauce and a little salt on the outside and under the skin.

Mix the flour, garlic, pepper, baking powder and seasoned salt together in a plastic bag or shallow tray.

Dip the chicken first into the beaten egg, then in the flour.

Fry in hot oil, turning frequently to prevent sticking and burning.

CARIBS AND BAR-B-Q

So far we have met the peaceful Arawaks who were quietly developing the original Caribbean culture when they were not running for their lives. I have briefly mentioned the savage, cannibalistic Caribs after whom the Caribbean was named and who just loved to eat the Arawaks. These guys were the alter-ego of the Arawaks. Where the Arawaks used conch shells and stones to make tools and jewellery, the Caribs made bludgeons by sticking the same items of culture and beauty into clubs. While the Arawaks were discovering how to process a dangerous poison into a preservative, the Caribs were using this same manioc poison to put on the tip of their weapons and kill their enemies.

I bet you're wondering why I am spending so much time on them. Well, for one thing, the Caribs to their credit, unlike their Arawak counterparts, actually survived the European invasion and to this day exist in Dominica and Trinidad. They were feared by their enemies and were willing to commit suicide – as they did at Sauteurs in Grenada when several of them jumped from a 100 foot cliff rather than surrender (to the French in this case).

As far as cooking is concerned, the Caribs gave the world one of its favourite outdoor activities – the barbecue. For, like it or not, a few hundred years ago, the treasured barbecue was used by the Caribs to cook the juicy Arawaks.

The Caribs as it turned out didn't have very nice table manners and it is no wonder that many barbecued meats seem to taste a lot better stolen off the fire and eaten with your hands.

BAR-B-Q CHICKEN

INGREDIENTS

4 chicken drumsticks

4 chicken thighs

2 cups Bar-B-Q Marinade (see
recipe on page 124)

Serves 4

METHOD

Wash and clean the chicken removing any excess fat or skin.
Squeeze out the excess water, then place in a bowl and cover with
marinade. (Make sure that the chicken is completely covered.)
Place it in the refrigerator and leave for at least 5 hours.

Grill over glowing coals.

BASSA BASSA CHICKEN

The combination of flavours in this dish really complement each other. I personally prefer the grilled version.

INGREDIENTS

4 chicken drumsticks

4 chicken thighs

1 tbs seasoned salt

1 six ounce jar Bassa Bassa Sauce
    or Tamarind Sauce (below)

Tamarind Sauce

4 oz fresh tamarinds

8 oz brown sugar

1 oz fresh minced garlic

½ tsp salt

1 tbs ground cumin

½ tsp minced Scotch bonnet *or*
    habanero pepper

1 cup boiling water

Serves 4

METHOD

Wash and clean the chicken pieces, removing any excess skin and fat. Pat them dry, then coat generously with the seasoned salt. Preheat the oven to 350 °F.

Place the chicken pieces in an oven-proof dish and bake for 30 minutes.

Baste each piece with Bassa Bassa Sauce or Tamarind Sauce and return to the oven for a further 15 minutes.

The chicken can also be grilled over glowing coals. Baste frequently with Bassa Bassa or Tamarind Sauce (see below.)

Tamarind Sauce

Soak the tamarinds in the boiling water for about 2 hours, then pulp them by squeezing and rubbing with your fingers. Try to remove all of the flesh from the seeds. Discard the seeds.

Stir in all the other ingredients. Refrigerate the unused portion for up to 3 months.

Bassa Bassa Chicken on a bed of red cabbage

CHICKEN CHOW MEIN

The Chinese came to the Caribbean as Indentured Servants after slavery was abolished. With them came their cuisine and this dish can be found in Jamaica, Trinidad and Guyana, where large Chinese communities exist to this day.

INGREDIENTS

2 lb Chinese egg noodles

1 chicken breast *boiled in salted water and shredded*

7 cloves garlic *minced*

½ tsp fresh ginger *minced*

2 tbs soy sauce

3 tbs sugar

¼ tsp salt

pinch MSG (optional)

1 can (16 oz) mixed vegetables

3 tbs vegetable oil

vegetable oil cooking spray

Serves 6

METHOD

Boil the noodles in salted water for 3 minutes, then drain and rinse under running water. Coat with cooking spray to prevent them from sticking together.

Heat the oil in a wok and stir-fry the garlic and ginger for 1 minute. Add the noodles, soy sauce, salt, sugar, and MSG, stirring all the time. Stir in the shredded chicken and mixed vegetables, then heat through.

Chicken Chow Mein garnished with red cabbage

GRENADA

Grenada is located in the Southern Caribbean. It is an island of lush green foliage where spices abound.

Grenada was first sighted and given the name Concepcion by Christopher Columbus during his third voyage in 1498 but his sailors called it Grenada since the mountains reminded them of the cliffs of Grenada in Spain and that name has remained with the island ever since. For many years after it was sighted, Grenada was avoided by the Europeans, mainly due to the fact that it was fairly well inhabited by the fierce Caribs, who in the early 1600s had already sent some British settlers fleeing for their lives. However, in 1650 some brave (maybe more stupid than brave) Frenchmen bribed their way ashore and so the first European settlement of Grenada occurred. As expected, the Caribs soon grew tired of sharing their island with the French and the battle began. In 1651 the Caribs were finally overcome and at Le Morne de Sauteur in Northern Grenada they valiantly chose to die rather than surrender. Some Caribs, including men, women and children jumped to their deaths off what was to become known as Leapers Hill. As with several other Caribbean islands, possession of Grenada was an on-going affair with the island constantly changing hands between the English and French. This continued until 1783 when the Treaty of Versailles awarded Grenada to Britain.

Interesting fact about Grenada

- This tiny Caribbean island with a population of approximately 109,000 produces a third of the world's nutmeg supply.

CHICKEN SALAD

This recipe comes from the island of Grenada and demonstrates the versatility of breadfruit once more.

INGREDIENTS

2 chicken breasts

1 breadfruit

½ cup mayonnaise

1 can (16 oz) mixed vegetables

1 small onion *chopped*

½ oz fresh parsley *chopped*

seasoned salt *to taste*

Serves 4

METHOD

Peel and boil the breadfruit in salted water until tender. This should take approximately 15 minutes. Dice the breadfruit in ¾ inch cubes and allow to cool.

Boil the chicken breasts in salted water, then cut them up into small pieces.

In a large bowl, mix all of the ingredients together. Cover and refrigerate for at least 1 hour before serving.

Chicken Salad with Marinated Carrots

CHICKEN CURRY

Chicken Curry and Roti with Channa Curry (garnished with strips of red and green pepper)

Every island has their version of curry. This version comes from Trinidad and is truly Caribbean. The East Indians came to this part of the world after slavery was abolished. Their cuisine went through a metamorphosis and the curry that we cook today bears no resemblance to the ones from India and Pakistan.

This is truly a 'Caribbean Treasure'!

The secret to making a really special curry is to stir-fry the dry powder for a few seconds before adding the meat. This process releases the curry flavour which is then absorbed in full by the meat.

INGREDIENTS

2 lb chicken breast *cut into bite-sized pieces*

4 potatoes *peeled and diced*

1 large onion *chopped*

1½ oz curry powder

3 tbs minced cilantro (coriander)

6 cloves garlic *minced*

½ tsp hot pepper sauce

1½ tsp salt *or to taste*

3 cups water

¼ cup vegetable oil

Secret Ingredient 3 tbsp Tamarind Paste

1 large green mango *diced, or* 3 tbsp lemon juice.

Serves 4

METHOD

Heat the oil in a saucepan and then add the onion and garlic. Stir-fry for 2 minutes or until the onions go limp. Add the salt and curry powder and continue stir-frying for about 10 seconds more. Add the meat and stir to coat with the curry mixture. Cover the saucepan and leave to cook for about 5 minutes, stirring at least twice during this time.

Add the water, pepper sauce, Tamarind Paste and potatoes and continue to cook on medium heat until the potatoes are soft and the meat is fully cooked. This should take approximately 25 minutes.

Serve with roti or over hot, boiled rice.

Notes:

Cooking tip: When using lemon juice, do not add until the final 10 minutes of cooking. The reason for this is that the lemon juice prevents the potatoes from becoming soft.

Tamarind paste can be bought in an Asian market.

ROTI

Curried meat, fish or chicken is almost always eaten with roti. In Trinidad and Tobago the traditional name is 'buss-up-shut', which translates into burst-up-shirt. This is because the cooked dough is hit with a wooden paddle and the end result looks like a shirt that has been shredded.

In Guyana the same roti is referred to as 'fling up and clap', because, instead of using a paddle, the hot roti is removed from the griddle and immediately tossed into the air. On the way down it is clapped (applause) once and thrown into the air again. This is repeated about four times. This process makes the roti soft, flaky and easy to tear and dip into the curry.

Some people prefer to keep the roti in its solid state which resembles a flour tortilla. The curry is then placed in the middle and rolled up in a similar way to the Mexican 'burrito'.

INGREDIENTS

1½ lb all-purpose flour

¼ cup vegtable oil

½ tsp salt

3 tsp baking powder

1¼ cups water

¼ cup margarine mixed with ¼ cup
    vegetable oil

METHOD

Mix the flour, baking powder and salt together. Mix in the water to form a dough, then knead in the ¼ cup oil, a little at a time. Divide this mixture into 5 pieces.

Knead each piece using a little more flour, then roll into a 6 inch circle. Baste it with the margarine and oil mix and sprinkle with a pinch of plain flour. Cut a slit from the centre of the circle to the outer edge and roll the dough to form a cone. Punch in the top with your index finger, cover with a damp cloth and allow the roti to stand for 30 minutes. Repeat for the other four.

Heat a griddle and brush it with oil. Roll the roti as flat as you possibly can, using a floured rolling pin and a floured surface. Cook on the hot griddle for about 1 minute each side, turning twice and basting each side with the margarine and oil mixture.

Remove from the griddle and 'fling up and clap' or hit with a paddle for 'buss-up-shut'.

(See photo, page 51.)

FRICASSÉE CHICKEN

The French are known for 'browning down' their meat and this recipe from Martinique is a typical example of that technique.

INGREDIENTS

1 large chicken *cut into about*
    10–12 pieces
1 tbs vegetable oil
2 tbs brown sugar
1 large onion *minced*
4 green onions *minced*
4 tomatoes *peeled and chopped*
2 cups water *or* chicken stock
½ tsp hot pepper sauce

Marinade
juice of 1 lime
4 cloves garlic *minced*
1 tsp thyme
1 tsp marjoram
1 tsp hot pepper sauce
3 tbs Worcestershire sauce
seasoned salt *to taste*

Serves 6

METHOD

Make the marinade by mixing all the ingredients together. Place the chicken in the marinade and steep for 2 hours. Drain and reserve marinade.

In a large saucepan, heat the oil and add the brown sugar, stirring all the time. The sugar will begin to caramelise. Do not let it burn. At this point add the drained chicken and brown for 15 minutes stirring constantly. Remove from the pan and set aside.

Sauté the onion and green onions in the juices left in the pan, then stir in the tomatoes and cook for 5 minutes. Pour over the water (or stock) and reserved marinade, then add the pepper sauce. Return chicken to the pan and simmer for 30 minutes or until it is tender. Adjust seasonings to taste.

Serve over boiled rice.

THE COMMONWEALTH OF DOMINICA

Dominica is the largest and most mountainous of the Windward Islands. Although the official language is English, most Dominicans are quick to revert to their own 'Creole' language when they are speaking to each other. This in itself gives an immediate insight into the history of the island which, like many others, was at the centre of a continuous tug-of-war for ownership between the English and French colonial powers.

In today's world of invented tourist attractions, Dominica's attractions are totally natural, with its tropical rainforest, rivers, numerous crater lakes and waterfalls. In case you haven't guessed by now, Dominica is a volcanic island. Its mountainous landscape extends deep into the ocean making this island particularly interesting to divers and even more so to the several Sperm whales who now contribute even further to Dominica's worldwide recognition as a prime destination for the eco-tourist.

Interesting facts about Dominica
- Dominica's boiling lake is one of the largest of its kind in the world.
- Unlike many other islands, the Caribs still exist here today. They were assigned their own territory – a 'massive' 3700 acres – in 1903, and approximately 3000 Caribs live there now.

MOUNTAIN CHICKEN

Actually, the mountain chicken referred to in this recipe is really a species of frog found on the islands of Dominica and Montserrat. In Dominica it is very expensive and can be found on the menu in many of the finest restaurants.

INGREDIENTS

1½ lb frogs' legs

2 large onions *sliced*

8 cloves garlic *minced*

1 large tomato *chopped*

1 tbs Worcestershire sauce

½ tsp hot pepper sauce

seasoned salt *to taste*

3 tbs ketchup

1½ cups water

4 tbs butter

4 tbs flour

1 green onion *chopped*

Serves 4

METHOD

Wash and clean the mountain chicken, then pat it dry with a paper towel. Rub with the seasoned salt, garlic, Worcestershire sauce, pepper sauce and ketchup, and set aside.

Heat the butter in a saucepan and sauté the onions for 3 minutes or until they become transparent, then add the tomato. Continue to cook for a further 3 minutes before adding the mountain chicken. Allow it to stew in its own juices for 10 minutes, stirring constantly.

Remove the mountain chicken, onion and tomato from the pan and stir in the flour, making sure to break up any lumps. A balloon whisk is ideal for this job. Pour in the water and bring the gravy to the boil. Return the mountain chicken, onion and tomato to the pan, adjust the seasonings to taste and allow the stew to simmer for 30 minutes or until the meat is tender. It may be necessary to add a little water as the stew cooks.

Sprinkle over the green onion before serving with peas and rice.

LIMA BEANS AND MINCED CHICKEN

This recipe came to me via a friend who lives in Grenada …
I hope you enjoy it!

INGREDIENTS

8 oz minced chicken

1 cup lima beans *soaked in water*
overnight, or 2 cups canned
variety

1½ tsp mixed herbs (thyme,
marjoram, oregano and basil)

½ tsp seasoned salt

1 onion *sliced*

4 cloves garlic *minced*

½ tsp hot pepper sauce

3½ cups water

½ cup of medium *or* sweet white
wine

¾ cup tomato sauce

2 tbs Worcestershire sauce

Serves 4

METHOD

Place the lima beans in a pan with water, wine, onion, garlic, pepper sauce, mixed herbs and seasoned salt, and boil until the beans are tender. Add more water if necessary.

Add the chicken, Worcestershire sauce and tomato sauce, adjust seasonings to taste and simmer for 25 minutes.

Serve with boiled rice or pasta.

(See **Note** on page 33 re cooking peas/beans).

Lima Beans and Minced Chicken, Candied Sweet Potatoes and boiled rice with red rose and orange centre on top

ST KITTS AND NEVIS

St Kitts and Nevis are located in the Northern Leeward Islands and are separated from each other by two miles of water. The central portion of St Kitts features a mountain range and a dormant volcano, Mount Liamuiga – which was the name given to the islands by its original inhabitants – the Caribs – and means 'Fertile Island'. The mountain is covered by dense tropical forests and the coastline is ringed by mostly black volcanic beaches, although a few beaches and most of those in Nevis feature golden sand.

St Kitts and Nevis have a combined population of approximately 44,000. The islands became independent from Britain in September 1983. The capital of St Kitts is Basseterre while that of Nevis is Charlestown.

St Kitts was sighted by Columbus on his second voyage in 1493. He originally named the island St Christopher after the patron saint of travellers, however the island became known as St Kitts over the years. Nevis was so named because its mist-covered mountain reminded Columbus of snow.

In 1623 St Kitts became the first Caribbean island to be colonised by the English with the arrival of Sir Thomas Warner. On arrival the colonists found the island already inhabited by the fierce Caribs. Fortunately for the settlers, the Carib chief Tegreman decided to make friends rather than wage war. This shared existence continued for the next year, at which time the English allowed some French sailors (survivors from a battle with the Spanish) to land on St Kitts. The Caribs obviously started to get worried about the increasing number of foreigners on their island and decided to attack them. The attack was well planned with support rounded up from the neighbouring islands. However they were betrayed by one of their women, and a combined force of French and English attacked the Carib settlement ambushing those from the other islands as they lay in wait near the mouth of a river. Those who weren't slaughtered fled to other islands.

Inevitably, it wasn't long before the French and English were at war with each other. As with many Caribbean islands, the ownership continuously changed from French to English until the Treaty of Versailles in 1783 formally ceded Nevis and St Kitts to the British.

Interesting fact about St Kitts
   • St Kitts was the first British colony in the Caribbean.

PINEAPPLE CHICKEN

If you like Chinese food, this Caribbean/Chinese favourite will surely hit the right spot!

INGREDIENTS

1 lb chicken breast *cut into bite-sized pieces*

2 tsp fresh grated ginger

4 cloves garlic *minced*

4 tbs vegetable oil

1 cup chopped onions

2 tbs tomato paste

2 tbs soy sauce

½ tsp seasoned salt

1 cup chicken stock *or* 1 chicken cube *dissolved in 1 cup of water*

1 cup sliced red and green peppers

1 cup pineapple juice

1½ cups pineapple chunks

2 tbs cornstarch *mixed in ¼ cup water*

2 tbs sugar

Serves 4

METHOD

Rub the chicken with the seasoned salt and set aside.

Heat the oil and sauté the ginger, garlic and onions for about 2 minutes.

Add the chicken, soy sauce and tomato paste and continue to stir-fry for approximately 5 minutes.

Pour in the chicken stock, pineapple juice, pineapple chunks, sugar and peppers and simmer on medium heat for about 15 minutes.

Stir the cornstarch mixture and add to the pan, stirring until it bubbles and thickens.

Pineapple Chicken garnished with red bell peppers

ROAST CHICKEN
AND STUFFING

Sundays are very special in many islands. A large meal is usually prepared and the entire family gathers to share it. This recipe is popular at such events in many of the islands.

INGREDIENTS

1 whole chicken (with giblets)

2 limes *juiced*

2 tsp salt

1½ tbs seasoned salt

1 tsp ground sage

Stuffing

giblets from the chicken

8 soda crackers

4 slices bread

2 tbs Barbadian Seasoning (see page 123)

3 tbs Worcestershire sauce

2 tbs tomato ketchup

1 tsp seasoned salt

½ tsp hot pepper sauce

½ tsp thyme

½ tsp basil

1 tbs vegetable oil

Serves 6

METHOD

Wash and clean the chicken removing any excess fat. Squeeze the lime juice on to the chicken and rub in the salt. Leave to stand for 10 minutes, then rinse and pat dry. Rub with the seasoned salt and sage. Make sure the seasoning gets under the skin where possible.

Place the stuffing (see below) into the cavity of the bird and close with skewers or needle and thread.

Dot with butter, cover with foil and roast in a preheated oven at 350 °F for 1 hour and 15 minutes. Baste every 20 minutes.

For the final 15 minutes uncover and allow the meat to brown.

Note:

1 hour and 15 minutes is usually enough to cook a 3–4 pound chicken.

Stuffing

Chop the giblets into small pieces and season with the Barbadian Seasoning and ketchup.

Soak the crackers and bread in a little water for a few minutes to soften.

Heat the oil and sauté the giblets in a pan for about 5 minutes. Pour in 2 cups water and simmer for 20 minutes. Squeeze out any excess water from the crackers and bread and add to the pan. Reduce the heat and season with pepper sauce, Worcestershire sauce, seasoned salt, basil and thyme. Stir constantly to prevent sticking. Add a little water if the mixture appears too stiff. Cook for about 5 minutes to blend flavours.

pork

SUNDAY LUNCH

One of the many traditions that have continued in Barbados to this day is that of having an extremely large Sunday lunch followed by an even better Sunday afternoon nap!

It is a real treat to drive through any neighbourhood on Sunday morning and enjoy the smells that permeate the atmosphere as the several households proceed to prepare a feast fit for a king.

A typical lunch could consist of:

– Pickled Cucumbers (Avocado)
– Sweet Potato Pie
– Tropical Coleslaw
– Peas and Rice
– Lettuce and Tomatoes
– Plantains in a Cheese Sauce
– Roast Chicken and Stuffing
– Roast Pork

The meal is normally served with soda mixed with coconut water or mauby, a favourite local drink made from the bark of a tree that came from Africa during the slave days.

Preparation of the Sunday lunch usually begins the night before when the pork and chicken are soaked in lime and salt, and the dried pigeon peas are soaked in water.

In colonial days it was mandatory to go to church on Sundays and the plantation owners would return home to a feast of even greater proportions usually prepared by the slaves.

Today the feast is prepared by a family member, usually the mother or an older daughter, who remains at home while the rest of the family go to church. On their return other members of the family would assist in the finishing touches of the Sunday lunch.

By the time the table is laid and the mountain of food consumed, it is time for an afternoon nap. Later in the afternoon there is sure to be a game of cricket or some other sport to pass the time.

Sunday is the day most Caribbean people worship, and the Caribbean has always been known for its religious tolerance. Barbados in particular, since it was settled, has been home to Hugenots, Methodists, Quakers, Catholics, Jews, and followers of the Church of England. While some of these religions no longer exist, the island is presently home to Anglicans, Jehovah's Witnesses, Muslims, Seventh Day Adventists, Bahais, Mormons, Buddhist, Pentecostals, and numerous other smaller religious groups along with the original Methodists, Catholics and Jews. As a matter of fact Barbados boasts having one of the oldest synagogues in the Western Hemisphere and many visitors marvel at the large number of churches that dot the landscape, as these, coupled with the large numbers of rumshops, seem to illustrate the unending struggle between good and not so good.

BARBADIAN ROAST PORK

On Sundays this dish graces many a Barbadian table. The meat is usually bought fresh the day before and 'seasoned-up' overnight.

INGREDIENTS

3 lb pork roast

2 limes

2 tsp salt

4 tbs Barbadian Seasoning (see recipe on page 123)

2 tbs Worcestershire sauce

Serves 8

METHOD

Wash the pork and rub with the juice of the limes and the salt. Leave to stand for 15 minutes, then rinse and pat dry. Cut slits in the meat in at least six places. Go as deep as you can. Pack the slits with Barbadian Seasoning and rub the remainder on the outside of the meat. Rub in the Worcestershire sauce and add a little more salt if necessary. (This is to your personal taste.)

Place in an oven-proof dish, skin side up, and bake for the first 30 minutes in a very hot oven (450 °F).

Reduce the heat to 350 °F.

Remove the roast from the oven, baste, cover with foil and continue to roast until done. This should take approximately 1¼ hours.

BAR-B-Q PIG-TAILS

Not for those watching their fat intake ... These tails are s-o-o-o-o good! They are commonly sold by vendors at the street corners in Barbados after sunset.

Pigs-tails offer a nice variation to any Bar-B-Q. If you are not too squeamish you'll find that they taste superb. I prefer to use the leaner parts of the tail and as my recipe calls for cured tails (which have been soaked in Brine) it is necessary to reduce the salt content before anything else can be done.

INGREDIENTS

4 cured pork tails

½ cup Bassa Bassa Sauce (Bar-B-Q Sauce can be used if Bassa Bassa is not available)

Serves 2

METHOD

Soak the tails in boiling water for at least 6 hours. Drain, then boil in fresh water for 30 minutes. Do not boil for longer because they tend to become too soft and fall apart on the grill.

Drain and baste them with the Bassa Bassa Sauce.

Grill on an outdoor barbeque or in the oven, turning frequently and basting with more sauce, as necessary.

Remember the meat is already cooked so it only needs about 15 minutes on the grill.

Note:

I have cooked pig-tails both on the grill and in the oven and my preference is for the grill. However, they taste quite good done in the oven and I have friends that prefer them this way – take your pick.

BASSA BASSA PORK

Tamarinds came to the Caribbean from India and are widely used in cooking, drinks and confectionery throughout the region. They add a very unique taste to this dish. If Bassa Bassa Sauce is not available use the recipe for Tamarind Sauce on page 47. Tamarinds are found in many Asian markets.

INGREDIENTS

8 pork hocks about 1½ inch thick

1 tbs seasoned salt

¼ cup oil

4 cups water

6 oz jar Bassa Bassa Sauce

2 tbs cornstarch (optional)

Serves 4

METHOD

Rub the pork hocks with seasoned salt and set aside.

Heat the oil in a saucepan and stir-fry the hocks for about 10 minutes.

Pour over the water and boil for 1 hour or until the hocks are tender and the meat separates from the bone easily. Add more water as necessary, but when they are nearly tender allow almost all of the water to evaporate.

Pour over the Bassa Bassa Sauce (or Tamarind Sauce – for recipe see page 47) and simmer for 10 minutes. Thicken with cornstarch dissolved in a little water.

PUDDIN' AN' SOUSE ON SAR'DAY
(PUDDING AND SOUSE ON SATURDAY)

If you can imagine the way the plantocracy lived it up in the old days …

Sunday was the day of worship and the big lunch. To entertain their friends properly, the planters would butcher at least one pig on Saturday so that the meat would be nice and fresh to roast come Sunday morning. But there were several parts that weren't used, like the trotters, the head, the maw (stomach), the intestines and the blood – and these were given to the slaves.

With a little imagination and lots of pepper, this seemingly useless combination of waste, was turned into a meal that is relished by people of all races and classes in the Caribbean to this day. On Saturday afternoons everyone heads for the vendor who makes the Best Puddin' an' Souse in the island … and every island has at least 400 of them for every family has their favourite – the person who makes the best – and it takes a very brave soul to disagree because this is sure to result in a heated argument especially when two or more groups of people come together to spend the day. There is always a big debate as to who the Puddin' an' Souse should be bought from and it is not unreasonable for each group to go their separate ways to buy the good stuff.

But – getting back to the Puddin' an' Souse – to begin with the variations are as numerous as lotto combinations. There is black pudding, made with the blood, mixed with seasoned sweet potatoes or rice, or even bread. There is white pudding without the blood. There is cow souse and pig souse and even souse made from chicken's feet, but what makes the difference is the way they are seasoned.

While it is still traditional to use the disposable parts, the less adventurous can nonetheless enjoy souse on Sar'day by substituting choice cuts of meat.

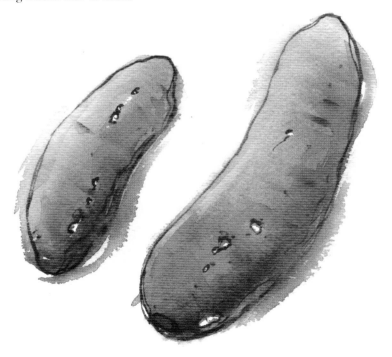

Souse and Pickled Breadfruit with Black Pudding

SOUSE AND PICKLED BREADFRUIT

Souse is traditionally eaten on Saturdays in islands like Trinidad and Tobago, Guyana, Barbados and Cayman along with black pudding which is made from the intestines and blood of the pig. The black pudding is prepared very differently in the various islands being stuffed with rice in Guyana, bread in Trinidad and sweet potato in Barbados, to name a few.

In this recipe, we will limit our meat to pork flap and not the parts that are traditionally used to make the souse.

The recipe consists of two parts: making the pickle and boiling the pork – so once you get the pork on the stove, you can go ahead and make the pickle.

INGREDIENTS

1 whole breadfruit *peeled and boiled in salted water*

3 lb pork flap

¼ cup fresh lime *or* lemon juice

salt *to taste*, approximately 3 tbs

salted water *to boil pork*

10 whole cloves

Pickle

5 small cucumbers *peeled*

4 medium onions *peeled*

½ Scotch bonnet *or* habanero pepper

2 oz fresh parsley

salt *to taste*

1½ cups fresh lime *or* lemon juice

½ tsp MSG (optional)

Serves 8

METHOD

Clean the pork flap and place in a pan with enough salted water to cover. Add the whole cloves and ¼ cup lime juice. Bring to the boil then reduce heat and simmer until the pork is tender. Drain, rinse in cold water and cut into bite-sized pieces.

Set aside to cool completely.

Note:

The pork must be completely cool before adding to the pickle – if not the pickle will look cooked.

Pickle

In a food processor place the onions, cucumbers, pepper and parsley. Process for 30 seconds – enough to give everything a coarse chop.

Make the pickle by blending the lime juice, salt and MSG with the chopped vegetables. Steep the pork in this mixture for at least one hour before serving.

Do not refrigerate as this will cause the pickle to jell.

Cube the breadfruit and add it to the pickle just before serving.

BLACK PUDDING
(BLOOD SAUSAGE)

This is the type of blood sausage that is popular in Guyana. On Saturdays many people leave their homes in search of 'Pudding and Souse'. Some restaurants serve this dish but usually the one that tastes the best is found in the homes of the old ladies that make it to sell to the local community.

INGREDIENTS

5 feet of sausage skin *cut into 30 inch pieces, or* 5 feet of pig intestines *cut into 30 inch pieces*

5 cups long grain rice *soaked in water for 2 hours*

2 cups coconut milk

5 cloves garlic *minced*

1 onion *chopped*

seasoned salt *to taste*

1 tbs hot pepper sauce

½ tsp basil

½ tsp thyme

½ tsp marjoram

¼ cup vegetable oil

2 cups pig's blood *strained*

Serves 8

METHOD

The intestines need to be thoroughly cleaned before they can be stuffed. Soak them in salt and lemon juice for 15 minutes and then turn them inside out and repeat. Rinse under running water.

Place the rice (drained), coconut milk, pepper sauce, herbs, onion and garlic in a saucepan with enough water to just cover the rice. Cover, bring to the boil, then reduce heat to lowest level and steam for 30 minutes or until all the water has evaporated.

Transfer the rice to a large bowl and mix in the vegetable oil and pig's blood. Adjust the seasonings to your taste. A sprinkle of herbs, a little pepper sauce and some seasoned salt usually does the job quite nicely.

Stuffing the skins …

Tie one end of the intestine with string and stuff it with rice using the handle of a wooden spoon and a funnel. Do not pack it too tightly as the mixture will expand during cooking and burst the skin. Tie the other end. Repeat with the other length of intestine.

Cut a 2 inch diameter hole in the centre of a 9 inch foil pie pan. Place it upside down in the bottom of a stockpot with about 1 gallon of water. Boil the water, then gently lower the sausages into the pot, reduce heat, cover and simmer for 30 minutes.

Remove the sausages to a platter and brush with vegetable oil. Slice into 1½ inch rounds and serve with souse and pickled breadfruit.

Note:

The sausage is cooked when an inserted toothpick comes out clean.

(For photo, see page 66.)

BREADFRUIT SALAD

This is from the island of St Lucia. Breadfruit is so widespread throughout the Caribbean islands that the variety of ways in which it is used seems endless ...

INGREDIENTS

1 breadfruit *peeled and boiled in salted water*

2 cucumbers *peeled and seeds removed*

5 cloves minced garlic

2 red bell peppers *seeds removed*

¼ cup fresh lime juice

1 lb cured pig-tails (salt pork or ham will do)

¼ tsp minced habanero or Scotch bonnet pepper

1 oz fresh parsley *minced*

salt *to taste*

Serves 6

METHOD

If using cured pig-tails, soak them in boiling water for at least 8 hours. Drain, and boil in fresh water for 30 minutes. Chop the tails into 1 inch pieces. Ham only needs to be diced in ½ inch cubes.

In a large bowl, dice the breadfruit and cucumbers in ¼ inch cubes. Julienne the bell peppers.

Mix all of the remaining ingredients together and allow the salad to marinate for at least 1 hour before serving.

GARLIC PORK

This recipe was brought to Guyana by the Portuguese. Breakfast on Christmas day would not be the same without Garlic Pork and Pepperpot. This is a classic example of how the cuisine has married over the years. Pepperpot came from the Arawak Indians. In Haiti they make a similar dish called Griots de porc *which is served with Green Plantain Chips.*

INGREDIENTS

4 lb pork flap

2 pints vinegar

8 oz garlic *minced*

5 oz fresh thyme *pounded to release flavour*

habanero or Scotch bonnet peppers *to taste, minced*

6 whole cloves

2 tsp salt

Serves 10

METHOD

Cut the pork into bite-sized pieces and steep in a solution of ¼ pint vinegar and water for 1 minute. Lift out using a slotted spoon and place in a large glass bottle or jar. Do not touch the meat with your hand.

Mix together the garlic, peppers and thyme. Add to the rest of the vinegar. Stir in the salt and cloves. Pour over the pork making sure that there is enough liquid to cover it completely.

Leave to soak at room temperature for 4 days.

After this time, remove the pork with a slotted spoon from the jar and place in a frying pan with a little of the liquid and leave to boil until it evaporates. The fat on the pork should melt, supplying enough to fry until brown.

Note:

It is not necessary to fry the entire jar of pork at the same time. It can be done in small portions during the following week.

Pepperpot, Garlic Pork and Green Plantain Chips

BELIZE

British sailors settled on Belize (previously known as British Honduras) in 1683, 180 years after Columbus first sailed into the Bay of Honduras. But centuries before either the British or the Spanish set foot on Belize the country was home to a very advanced civilisation, the Maya Indians, whose scientific outlook on life led them to develop and use complex mathematics and numbering systems that equalled those developed much later in Europe.

By the time that Christopher Columbus set eyes on Belize, the Maya had long disappeared, and the British settlers who arrived much later should have been free to carry on their logging activities in the vast forests of the country. This was not to be, however, and the settlers had to put up with numerous attacks from their Spanish neighbours. The attacks continued until 1798 when British ships destroyed the Spanish Armada at the Battle of St Georges Caye.

In 1862 Britain declared Belize (then British Honduras) to be one of its colonies; it is for this reason that this Central American country is identified with the Caribbean unlike its Spanish-speaking neighbours, Mexico and Guatemala.

Interesting facts about Belize

- Located about 30 km offshore, Belize's barrier reef is second only to the great barrier reef of Australia.
- One of the most loved foods in the world – chocolate – was developed by the Maya. It was considered to be the 'food of the gods' and made available only to a privileged class.
- The majority of Belize's population had ancestors who were pirates-turned-loggers after piracy started to become too risky.

Cochinita Pibil in a banana leaf

COCHINITA PIBIL
(PIT-BAKED PORK)

A Mayan favourite from that ancient civilisation, Cochinita Pibil was originally made with wild boar and baked in a pit lined with stones and hot coals. The people of Belize prepare this dish today in much the same way as their ancestors did … with the exception of the pit.

INGREDIENTS

4–5 lb pork shoulder roast

2 tsp salt

3 tbs Seville orange juice *or* juice
   blend (*see below*)

2 large pieces of banana leaves
   *ducked in a pan of boiling water
   for 30 seconds to make them
   flexible*

Seasoning Paste

3 tbs ground annatto seeds

2 tsp oregano

2 bay leaves

1 tsp cumin seeds

1 inch stick cinnamon

4 whole cloves

3 whole allspice berries

15 whole black peppercorns

½ tsp paprika

2 tsp salt

10 cloves garlic *minced*

4 tbs Seville orange juice *or, if this is
   not available, mix together:*
   1 tsp grated grapefruit rind
   3 tbs orange juice
   3 tbs grapefruit juice
   2 tbs lime juice
   Leave to stand for 2 hours to allow
   the flavours to blend.
   Yield: ½ cup.

Serves 10

METHOD

To make the seasoning, place the cumin seeds, bay leaves, cinnamon, cloves, allspice and peppercorns in a coffee grinder. Process to a fine powder. Sift and reprocess if necessary. Blend in the other ingredients to make a thick paste.

Score the pork with a sharp knife and rub in the salt and juice. Coat the pork with the paste and wrap in the banana leaves.

Place the pork in a dish and refrigerate overnight or for at least 5 hours.

Lay a rack in the bottom of a large, covered roaster and place the pork on it. Pour in ½ cup water, cover tightly and roast in a preheated oven at 325 °F for 2 hours.

Remove the banana leaf, turn the meat, baste with the pan juices and continue roasting, covered, for another 2 hours. Baste at least twice during this time. The meat is finished when the juices run clear and it falls from the bone easily.

Remove the meat from the bone and shred roughly. Arrange on a platter and pour the pan juices over it.

Serve with warm tortillas and the salsa of your choice.

Note:
If possible make the seasoning paste at least 2 hours ahead in order to give the flavours a chance to combine.

HAM AND BLACKEYES IN COCONUT MILK

This is typical of a Caribbean dish ... where a little bit of meat goes a long way. Of course, the flavour is never sacrificed as you can tell by the seasonings used.

INGREDIENTS

1 cup blackeye peas *soaked in water overnight, or* 1 can (16 oz) canned variety

1 lb ham *cut into 1 inch cubes*

7 cloves garlic *minced*

1 large onion *chopped*

1 tsp thyme

1 tsp marjoram

½ tsp basil

1 tbs liquid smoke

1 tsp salt

1½ cups coconut milk

2 cups water

½ tsp hot pepper sauce

Serves 4

METHOD

Wash and drain the blackeye peas and place them in a pressure cooker together with the garlic, onion, thyme, marjoram, basil, salt, coconut milk and water. Cover and pressure-cook for 25 minutes. (If using canned peas simmer for 10 minutes.)

Allow the pressure to dissipate, then open the cooker and add the ham and pepper sauce. Add a little water if it is too thick.

Simmer for 10 minutes then adjust the seasonings, for example, add more herbs or pepper sauce.

Simmer for another 10 minutes. Stir in the liquid smoke and cook for 1 more minute.

Serve with boiled rice.

Ham and Blackeye Peas in Coconut Milk with star shaped okra in the middle

HAM WITH SCALLOPED YAMS

All of the islands have root crops (ground provisions) featuring prominently in their cuisine. The yams are usually very large, about 5 to 8 pounds each and white on the inside. Almost any variety will produce a good result.

INGREDIENTS

3 lb yams

3 tbs margarine *melted*

1½ cups milk

breadcrumbs

salt and pepper *to taste*

1 onion *minced*

8 oz ham *cut into ¼ inch cubes*

Serves 4

METHOD

Peel the yams and cut in thin slices, about ½ inch thick.

Place a layer of the yams in a greased oven-proof dish, drizzle with margarine, sprinkle with breadcrumbs, onion, salt, pepper and cubes of ham. Repeat the layer ending with yams. Brush with margarine and sprinkle some breadcrumbs over. Pour over the milk, then cover and bake in a moderate oven for 1 hour.

Uncover and bake for a further 15 minutes, or until tender and brown.

RELIGION

Barbados was first colonised by the British in 1627 and remained a British colony until its independence on 30 November 1966.

From the early days of its settlement, the Church of England made its presence felt as it stood guardian over the colonists' morals. Blasphemy, which included the use of phrases containing the word 'God', helped to spawn one of the island's famous expressions – Gaw Bline ya – which translates to 'God Blind You' and is daily wished on friends and enemies alike. Back then blasphemy was punishable by a visit to the Pillory in Bridgetown where you were inevitably stoned or, if the crime warranted, even be branded on your cheek with a 'B' to show the world how sinful you were. In those days the law of the land stated that you had to go to church on Sundays and so, in the absence of newspapers or radio, the church was in the best position to communicate any current events, and to serve as the government's propaganda machine. The Church of England was by no means the only religion on the island at this time – Quakers and Methodists were also present though their followers were much fewer in number.

Barbados has always been known for its religious tolerance. The 1652 Charter of Barbados gave all individuals the right to believe in whatever religion they chose. Thus the Quakers were preaching against slavery in the midst of a population who made their wealth at the expense of the slaves and the Moravians from Germany came to Barbados with the main intention of converting the slaves. It was ironic that the slave trade which was propagated by the need for the large cheap labour force required to reap sugar cane, can be attributed to Dutch Jews who arrived in the island from Brazil and taught the planters how to cultivate that crop successfully.

In present-day Barbados, Catholics, Methodists, Moslems and Jews are numbered among the more than 100 religions whose followers co-exist peacefully on an island of only 166 square miles.

DREIZ et POIS du BOIS
PEAS & RICE WITH PORK

At Christmas time in Guadeloupe this dish can be found on many tables. The 'browning down' technique demonstrated in the stewing process is what makes the cooking of the French islands unique.

INGREDIENTS

2 lb stewing pork

2 tbs Barbadian Seasoning (see recipe on page 123)

2 tbs tomato ketchup

3 tbs vegetable oil

8 oz carrots *peeled and sliced*

3 potatoes *peeled and cubed*

seasoned salt *to taste*

1 tsp hot pepper sauce

Serves 8

METHOD

Wash and cut the pork into bite-sized pieces. Season with ketchup and Barbadian Seasoning. Heat the oil in a heavy skillet and stir-fry the pork on high heat. Add a few drops of water every few minutes and continue cooking. Stir frequently to prevent sticking. This method will allow the pork to brown naturally without the addition of caramel or 'browning'. Continue for 15 minutes.

Pour in 4 cups of water, the carrots, potatoes, pepper sauce and seasoned salt and simmer until the pork is tender. This should take approximately 30 minutes.

Serve with Peas and Rice (see recipe on page 145).

ANTIGUA

Christopher Columbus sighted Antigua on his second voyage in 1493 and named it after Santa Maria la Antigua. It took another century before any European settlement occurred since there wasn't much fresh water available. The island was finally colonised in 1632 and officially became a British colony in 1667. Initially tobacco was Antigua's main crop, however this was replaced by sugar with the inevitable result – the importation of African slaves.

Although many British captains used Antigua's harbour to repair their ships and for the protection it offered against hurricanes, it wasn't until 1725 that its importance as a home base for the Royal Navy in the Caribbean was recognised. With the never-ending battles between the Europeans in the Caribbean during that period, it was important that the British warships had a safe, protected harbour from which they could quickly respond to any threat, and Antigua's English harbour was perfect for the purpose.

The harbour served the Royal Navy faithfully for over 100 years until it was finally abandoned in 1899 having at last outlived its usefulness. During that period it had the honour of being commanded by none other than Horatio Nelson, who arrived in Antigua in 1784. It was from here that he sailed to the Battle of Trafalgar and into history.

Interesting facts about Antigua

- English harbour is now the only Georgian dockyard in the world.
- During Nelson's early days in Antigua, he had to remain on board his ship to avoid being arrested. He was being sued by the local merchants for the loss of business he created by enforcing a law which prevented them from trading with the Americans.

PEPPERPOT AND FUNGI
(COO-COO)

A favourite with Antiguans, this Pepperpot bears no relationship to the one made by the Arawaks.

INGREDIENTS

1 large bell pepper

10 oz fresh *or* frozen spinach

1 lb orkas

1 large eggplant

8 oz finger squash

2 christophenes

1 small green papaya

12 oz pumpkin

1 onion

8 cloves garlic

2 green onions

½ tsp hot pepper sauce

1 tsp thyme

8 oz salt pork

1 cup pigeon / blackeye peas *or* 1
    can (16 oz) canned variety

Dumplings
see page 16

Serves 6

METHOD

Wash, peel and cut up the vegetables. Place all the ingredients except the salt pork, pepper sauce and pigeon peas in a saucepan with salted water and boil for 15 minutes or until tender. Drain the vegetables, but do not discard the cooking liquid. Set aside.

Boil the peas in a separate pan until tender. Drain and set aside.

Cut up the salt pork and simmer for at least 30 minutes, or until tender. Drain, but do not discard the cooking liquid.

Mash the vegetables with a fork adding a little of the cooking liquid from the salt pork. Add the peas, pepper sauce and salt pork to the pan together with 1 cup of the vegetable cooking liquid. Bring to the boil, then add the dumplings. Adjust the seasonings to your taste and simmer for 15 minutes, adding liquid as necessary.

Serve with Coo-Coo. (see recipe on page 134)

(See **Note** on page 33 re cooking peas/beans.)

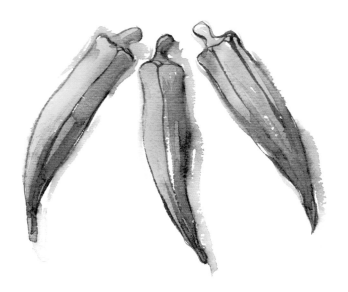

PORK WITH EGGPLANT

A really hearty stew from Martinique.

INGREDIENTS

2 tbs vegetable oil

3 tbs sugar

1 lb pork *cut into bite-sized pieces*

½ tsp marjoram

½ tsp basil

1 lb potatoes *peeled and diced*

1 large eggplant *peeled and diced*

1 onion *minced*

4 cloves garlic *minced*

1 tbs ground cumin

seasoned salt *to taste*

1 tsp hot pepper sauce

2½ cups water *or* stock

8 whole allspice berries

Serves 4

METHOD

Season the pork with the onion, garlic, cumin, herbs, seasoned salt and pepper sauce. Set aside.

Heat the oil in a saucepan and add the sugar stirring constantly until it starts to caramelise. Be careful not to burn it.

Add the pork and cook, stirring frequently for 10 minutes.

Add the eggplant, herbs, allspice and potatoes and cook for 3 more minutes. Pour over the water or stock and simmer for 45 minutes, or until tender. Adjust seasonings to taste, and serve.

Pork with Eggplant

PORK CHOPS WITH STUFFED GUAVAS

This is a wonderful 'special occasion' dish from Antigua. Guavas are usually sweet and the savoury stuffing together with the chops bring together an exotic Caribbean experience.

INGREDIENTS

4 large pork chops

1 tsp thyme

3 cloves garlic *minced*

seasoned salt and pepper *to taste*

juice of 1 lime

3 tbs guava jelly *or* jam

1 can guavas *drained and the juice reserved, or* 4 fresh guavas *cut in half*

1 tbs cornstarch

Stuffing

1 large onion *minced*

1½ cups breadcrumbs

1 tsp basil

1 tsp thyme

1 tbs fresh parsley *minced*

2 tbs rum

seasoned salt and pepper *to taste*

5 tbs butter

Serves 4

METHOD

Rub the chops with the thyme, garlic, salt and pepper, and set aside.

Place the lime juice, guava jelly and the reserved guava juice in a pan and heat for 2 minutes, until the jelly has melted. Set aside.

To make the stuffing, sauté the onion in 3 tablespoons butter for 2 minutes then add the breadcrumbs, basil, thyme, parsley and rum. Season to taste with seasoned salt and pepper.

Scoop out the seeds from the guavas and discard. Fill the cavities with the stuffing, and dot with butter.

Line a pan with foil and place the chops and guavas in it. Baste with a little of the guava juice, then broil on each side for 10 minutes brushing frequently with the juice.

Remove the guavas after the first 10 minutes. Continue to cook the chops until they are golden brown and done.

Place the chops and guavas on a serving platter.

Pour the pan juices into the pot with the melted jelly and heat until it boils. Mix the cornstarch with a little water and add to the pot. Cook for 1 minute until the sauce bubbles and thickens. Pour over the chops and guavas.

Serve immediately.

PORK CHOPS IN MANGO SAUCE

The tropical fruit sauce enhances the flavour of the pork. It packs just enough heat to make you take notice.

INGREDIENTS

4 large pork chops
3 cloves garlic *minced*
seasoned salt *to taste*

Mango Sauce
1 large mango *peeled, sliced and puréed in a blender with 1 cup water*
1 tbs minced raisins
3 cloves garlic *minced*
1 small onion *minced*
1 tsp fresh ginger *minced*
1 cup wine vinegar
½ tsp minced Scotch bonnet *or* habanero pepper
½ tsp salt
1 cup sugar
2 tbs cornstarch *dissolved in ¼ cup water*
½ tsp sesame oil

Serves 4

METHOD

Rub the chops with the garlic and seasoned salt, then set aside.

Place the chops in an oven-proof dish, and broil for 10 minutes on each side, or until fully cooked.

In the meantime make the sauce …
Place all the ingredients except the sesame oil and cornstarch in a pan and bring to the boil. Reduce the heat and simmer for 10 minutes. Pour in the cornstarch and simmer for a further minute. Stir in the sesame oil and turn off the heat.

Remove the chops to a serving platter and pour the sauce over them just before serving.

Pork Chops in Mango Sauce – slice of mango in the centre

SALT PORK

Many Caribbean dishes use salt pork or pigs-tails as part of their ingredients. In the days before refrigerators 'salting' meat was a way of preserving it. Although those times are long gone, the tradition lives on …

I always thought that this was truly a Caribbean thing but recently while speaking with a 'pig-tail' manufacturer in Florida I found out that the Hispanic community use salt pork and pig-tails in much larger quantities than we do.

INGREDIENTS

10 lb cured pig-tails *or* pork ribs

1 lb salt

1 tsp cinnamon

4 oz brown sugar

2 tsp salt petre

METHOD

Mix together the salt, sugar, cinnamon, and salt petre. Divide it into two equal parts.

Wipe the meat with a clean damp cloth and cut up into 2 inch pieces.

Rub the meat with half of the curing mix then pack it into a clean, covered container. Refrigerate for 1 week.

At the end of 1 week, rub the remaining curing mix into the meat and return to the refrigerator for a further 2 weeks. Turn twice during this time.

After 3 weeks the meat will be cured and can be used as required in the various recipes.

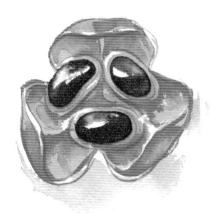

ACKEE AND SALTFISH

This is the national dish of Jamaica and is usually served with Festival – a kind of fried bread. Some friends of mine have tried it with Coo-Coo, the national dish of Barbados, and the two go very well together. I like to think of Ackee and Saltfish with Coo-Coo as 'Caribbean Unity'.

Although Ackee came from Africa, Jamaica is the only island in the Caribbean that eats it in any large quantity.

INGREDIENTS

1 can (16 oz) ackee *drained*

2 oz boneless salted cod

1 onion *chopped*

8 cloves garlic *minced*

2 medium tomatoes *chopped*

2 rashers bacon *or* Sizzlean *cut up*

1 tsp hot pepper sauce

3 tbs margarine

Serves 4

METHOD

Boil the salted cod for 5 minutes, then drain and cool under running water. Shred the fish with your fingers and set aside.

Next, heat the margarine in a pan, then add the onion and garlic. Sauté until the onion is transparent, then add the tomatoes, bacon and pepper sauce. Cook for a further 5 minutes.

Stir in the saltfish, cover and simmer for 3 minutes.

Add the ackee and, using a fork and very gentle movements, fold it in.

Cover and simmer for 10 minutes to allow the ackee to absorb the flavour. Add a little water if necessary.

Note:
The ackee in this dish is very fragile so it should be handled as little as possible. Stirring should only be done with a fork.

Ackee and Saltfish with Festival

FESTIVAL

This recipe was created by a Jamaican fisherman from Braeton, St Catherine, Jamaica. He combined the East Indian Roti with the Johnny Cake and came up with a fried bread that he tested at Hellshire Beach, a popular haunt for most Kingston dwellers.

He called his creation 'Festival' because 'Festival nice, just like Festival'.

Today Festival is legendary and is often served with Fried Fish, Jerked Pork or Chicken, Ackee and Saltfish, or simply by itself.

INGREDIENTS

9 oz flour

3 oz cornmeal

1 tsp baking powder

½ tsp salt

1 tbs sugar

2 tbs margarine

⅛ tsp ground cinnamon

⅛ tsp ground nutmeg

water

vegetable oil *for frying*

Serves 4

METHOD

In a bowl, cut the margarine into the flour then add all of the other ingredients. Slowly add enough water to moisten, then knead on a floured board for 5 minutes. Return the dough to the bowl and cover with a damp cloth for 15 minutes.

Divide the dough into 9 pieces and roll each piece into a sausage shape, then flatten.

Deep-fry until golden.

(For photo, see page 83.)

BAXTER'S ROAD

In Barbados fried fish and Baxter's Road are synonymous.

Vendors light up their huge coalpots from the early evening, and the fish fry continues until the early hours of the morning. When you have finished partying this is the place to visit for a nice piece of hot fish, straight out of the pan, and a cold beer.

Over the years Baxter's Road has become a favourite with many tourists, who enjoy the hot spicy steaks of fish as much as we do.

Larger fish that would normally be prepared in steaks are called steak fish to differentiate them from the smaller fish that would be prepared whole.

Despite the popularity of steak fish, flying fish, so named because of their ability to spread their fins and glide in the air for several yards when threatened, remain the overall favourite of Barbadians. These fish travel in schools and it is a fantastic sight to see several of them gliding through the air simultaneously.

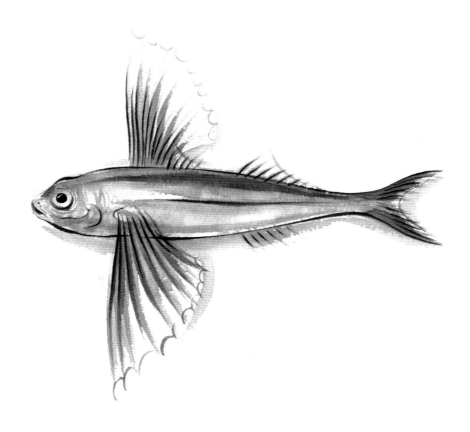

BARBADIAN FRIED FISH

INGREDIENTS

4 steaks white fish

1 lemon *or* lime

1 tsp salt

4 tbs Barbadian Seasoning (see
    recipe on page 123)

2 tbs Worcestershire sauce

4 cups all-purpose flour

5 tsp seasoned salt

2 tsp granulated garlic

2 tsp roasted cumin

2 tsp curry powder

2 cups milk

vegetable oil *for frying*

Serves 4

METHOD

Squeeze juice of the lime on to the fish and rub in the salt. Leave
to stand for 5 minutes.

Rinse and pat dry, then cut 2 slits in each piece of fish with a
sharp knife. Press the Barbadian Seasoning into the slits and rub
the remainder on the outside of the steaks.

Make a batter with the milk, 1 cup of flour, Worcestershire
sauce, 2 teaspoons seasoned salt, 1 teaspoon each of garlic, cumin
and curry.

Mix the remaining flour, garlic, cumin, curry and seasoned salt
together in a plastic bag or shallow tray.

Dip the fish first into the batter, then in the flour. Fry in hot
oil making sure to turn frequently to prevent sticking and
burning.

STEAMED FLYING FISH

Steamed Flying Fish and Coo-Coo is the national dish of Barbados. No visit to that island would be complete without a taste of this treat.

These fish which grow to around 15 inches long live on the surface of the ocean and do not actually fly. They leap into the air and spread their enlarged pectoral fins allowing them to glide over the ocean's surface with recorded distances of over 600 feet. However, the normal distance is around 30 feet.

INGREDIENTS

8 flying fish fillets

3 limes

1 tbs salt

3 tbs Barbadian Seasoning (see recipe on page 123)

1 large onion *sliced*

6 cloves garlic *minced*

1 green bell pepper *cut in julienne strips*

½ oz fresh thyme

½ oz fresh marjoram

1 tsp parsley *chopped*

1 large tomato *chopped*

1 tsp lime juice

2 cups water

½ tsp hot pepper sauce

½ tsp curry powder

3 tbs margarine

seasoned salt *to taste*

Serves 4

METHOD

Rub the fish with the juice of the limes and the salt and leave to stand for 10 minutes.

Rinse the fish and pat dry with paper towels, then rub in the Barbadian Seasoning. Roll each up (like a sausage) and secure with a toothpick.

Heat the margarine in a saucepan and sauté the onion and garlic for 3 minutes, or until the onions become transparent. Add the tomato and parsley and continue to cook for a further 2 minutes. Tie the thyme and marjoram together and add to the pan together with the remaining ingredients – except the fish. Bring to the boil, then reduce the heat and simmer for 10 minutes. Add the fish and continue to simmer for 10 minutes.

Serve with Coo-Coo (see page 134.).

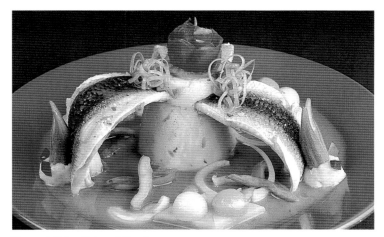

Steamed Flying Fish and Coo-Coo

FRIED or STUFFED FLYING FISH

Another way to prepare this Barbadian treasure!

INGREDIENTS

8 filleted flying fish

1 lime

½ tsp salt

3 tbs Barbadian Seasoning (see recipe on page 123)

1 egg *beaten*

1 tbs water

1 cup flour

1 cup breadcrumbs

½ tsp seasoned salt ⎫ *mixed*

½ tsp granulated garlic ⎭ *together*

2 ripe plantains *peeled and cut into 2 inch rounds*

vegetable oil *for frying*

Serves 4

METHOD

Squeeze the juice of the lime on to the fish and rub in the salt. Leave to stand for 5 minutes.

Rinse and pat dry, then rub the Barbadian Seasoning on the fish fillets. Use a generous amount of seasoning and try to get it into all the crevices.

Blend the water with the beaten egg.

Coat the fish with the flour, then the egg and lastly the breadcrumbs.

Fry in hot oil for about 2 minutes on each side.

To make the stuffed version. . .
Wrap each fish around a piece of plantain and secure with a toothpick.

Coat the fish in flour, egg and breadcrumbs, then deep-fry each fish for 3 minutes on each side.

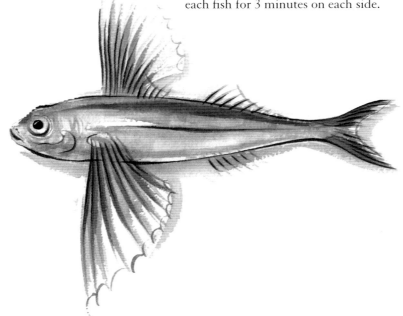

BAKED FISH WITH PINEAPPLE

Combining tropical fruit with seafood or meat is very popular in the Caribbean. The sweet and tangy flavour of the pineapple in this dish complements the fish nicely. All that's needed to complete this meal is a tall frosty glass of Pina Colada!

INGREDIENTS

1 lb white fish fillet *cut into 4 pieces*

2 tbs lime juice

½ tsp salt

¾ cup breadcrumbs

3 tbs Worcestershire sauce

1 tbs seasoned salt

2 large tomatoes *cut in wedges*

1 large onion *thinly sliced*

1 red bell pepper *cut in julienne strips*

½ cup pineapple juice

½ cup crushed pineapple

1 tbs margarine

Serves 4

METHOD

Rub the fish with lime juice and salt and leave to stand for 5 minutes.

Rinse and pat dry, then rub with the seasoned salt and Worcestershire sauce. Coat with breadcrumbs and place in a shallow oven-proof dish that has been greased with the margarine. Bake in a preheated oven at 350 °F for 20 minutes.

Arrange the tomato wedges, onion, bell pepper and pineapple on top of the fish. Pour on the pineapple juice and return to the oven for another 20 minutes.

Serve with boiled pasta.

BULJOL – PICK UP SALTFISH

When having a drink in Trinidad or the Virgin Islands this salad is served on crackers and is a most welcome snack. It is also served as a side dish, and sometimes even for breakfast. When avocados are in season, they are sliced and arranged around the Buljol.

INGREDIENTS

8 oz boneless salted cod fish

2 tbs fresh lime juice

2 cucumbers *peeled and diced*

1 onion *chopped*

3 cloves garlic *minced*

1 green pepper *seeded and cut in julienne strips*

3 tomatoes *chopped*

3 tbs olive oil

3 tbs fresh minced parsley

¼ tsp Scotch bonnet *or* habanero pepper *minced*

3 hard-boiled eggs

Serves 4

METHOD

Boil the fish in water for 5 minutes. Drain and flake the fish, with your fingers.

Add the lime juice, garlic, hot pepper, parsley, cucumber, onion, green pepper and tomatoes to the fish and mix together.

Stir in the oil. Garnish with the sliced hard-boiled eggs.

Refrigerate for at least 2 hours before serving.

Buljol and crackers with cucumber

TRINIDAD AND TOBAGO

Trinidad

Trinidad was 'discovered' by Columbus on 31 July 1498 on his third voyage. He called the island La Trinidad, in honour of the Holy Trinity, to whom he no doubt felt very indebted at the time, since he had spent the previous week stuck in the doldrums (an area located between latitudes 30 degrees north and 30 degrees south, in the vicinity of the equator, which typically has calm or light winds). As was customary he claimed the island for Spain and, as per usual, the attempts to subdue the original Amerindian inhabitants took the path of forced conversion to Christianity, enslavement, disease and near annihilation.

Trinidad remained largely uncolonised until 1783, when the King of Spain issued the historic Cedula-of-Population, which offered free land to any Roman Catholic who resided in any country friendly to Spain.

Most of the new colonists were French who, with free blacks, flocked to Trinidad from the neighbouring islands. Because extra land was granted for each slave owned, the population of Trinidad jumped from approximately 3000 in 1783 to almost 18,000 in 1789, with over 10,000 being slaves. The rich mixture of races and culture continued in Trinidad with the arrival of the British who, in 1797, conquered the island for Britain.

With the abolition of slavery on 1 August 1834, Trinidad planters were faced with a dilemma. Their fortunes were totally dependent on free slave labour which they would no longer have at their disposal. The first attempt to appease the planters was decreed by Britain. 'Ex-slaves' would be obliged to serve a four to six year period of apprenticeship with their former owners. This meant that slavery, though officially abolished, could continue under a different name.

The planters appointed an agent for immigration responsible for finding cheap alternatives to the slave labour. This resulted in the recruitment of Portuguese, freed Africans and various other groups, with little success, followed by Indians. The planters found the Indian workers to be perfect for the job at hand and the Indian population in Trinidad soon jumped from 200 in 1845 to over 140,000 by 1917.

Today those of East Indian and African origin represent, respectively, 36 per cent and 46 per cent of Trinidad's total population and these, together with the Chinese, who arrived between 1848 and 1852, helped to complete the mixture of races and culture for which Trinidad is renowned.

Tobago

Tobago is often referred to as 'Robinson Crusoe Island'. It got its name from the Carib word 'Tavaco', a pipe used by the Amerindians to smoke tobacco leaves. It was inhabited by Caribs in 1498 but these were all killed by 1632 when the first Dutch Settlers arrived.

Tobago was constantly fought over, changing hands frequently until 1814 when it finally became a British colony. With the abolition of slavery Tobago's sugar industry eventually failed and in 1888 it was annexed to Trinidad by the British Government, creating the state of Trinidad and Tobago.

Interesting facts about Trinidad and Tobago

- The first oil well in the world was drilled in Trinidad in 1857.
- The pitch lake in Trinidad is the source of the world's largest supply of natural bitumen.
- Trinidad is credited with the only non-electronic musical instrument invented this century. It is the 'steel pan', which is made from huge oil drums, tuned to reproduce the musical scale.
- Tobago was the most fought-over island in the Caribbean.

CALLALOO AND CRAB

This is the national dish of Trinidad and Tobago. Traditionally, whole crabs are used but if they are not available crab meat will produce just as good a result.

Some people dislike picking the meat from the shell – my husband is one of those, he says it's too much work.

INGREDIENTS

1½ lb frozen *or* fresh spinach
   (callaloo)

15 okras *cut into cartwheels*

1 onion *diced*

10 cloves garlic *minced*

1 tomato *chopped*

salt *to taste*

1 tsp hot pepper sauce

MSG *to taste* (optional)

4 tsbs cilantro (coriander) *minced*

1 tsp mixed herbs

2 tbs vegetable oil

1 cup coconut milk

1 lb crab meat *or* 8 whole crabs
   backs removed and cleaned

Serves 4

METHOD

Stir-fry the onion and garlic in oil for two minutes, then add the tomato and continue to cook for a further minute.

Add the callaloo and okras, salt, pepper sauce, herbs, cilantro and MSG. Stir-fry for about 3 minutes more.

Add the coconut milk and simmer for 15 minutes. Using a wire whisk or swizzle, stir vigorously to mash the callaloo. Next, add the crab, adjust seasonings to your taste and continue to simmer for a further 15 minutes. Add a little water if necessary.

Serve over boiled rice, or as a side dish.

COCONUT SHRIMP

The coconut milk, mangoes and cilantro (coriander) make this an outstanding 'special occasion' dish. Whenever I make this recipe there never seems to be enough to go around – it just disappears...

INGREDIENTS

2 cups coconut milk

4 tbs margarine

8 garlic cloves *minced*

2½ lb medium *cooked* shrimp

1 large onion *minced*

2 tbs fresh ginger *minced*

3 tbs fresh cilantro *minced*

1½ tsp seasoned salt

3 tbs cornstarch *dissolved in*
  ¼ cup water

1 large ripe mango *peeled and diced*

Serves 6

METHOD

Sauté the onion, garlic and ginger in the margarine for 2 minutes, then stir in the coconut milk, the cilantro and mango. Cover and simmer for 8 minutes. Add a little seasoned salt to taste.

Finally stir the cornstarch mixture and add to the pot together with the cooked shrimp. Cook until the sauce bubbles and thickens – about 1 minute.

Serve over warm pasta.

Coconut Shrimp

THE BAHAMAS

The Bahamas consist of approximately 700 islands of various sizes covering over 100,000 square miles of the Atlantic, the main islands being Andros, New Providence (where the capital Nassau is located), Grand Bahama, Eleuthera, Great Abaco, and Great Inagua.

It was on San Salvador Island in the Bahamas that Christopher Columbus first set foot in the 'New World' on 12 October 1492.

From that time onwards, the history of the Bahamas reads like a best-selling novel…

The arrival of the Spanish conquistadores who followed Columbus to the New World around 1500 signalled an end to the peaceful lives of the Arawaks who were the original inhabitants of the Bahamas. For the conquistadores, with their hearts set only on amassing huge fortunes, the Arawaks provided the cheapest possible form of labour – slave labour. The slaves were forced to harvest pearls and work in the mines of Cuba and several other islands; however they were quickly annihilated by European diseases. With the end of the slave labour, the Spanish left the Bahamas – never to look back – and the history of the Bahamas was left to be written by English settlers and notorious pirates.

British settlers first came to the island of Eleuthera in 1648 and quickly established a solid agricultural base on the island.

But while the settlers were busy exploiting the land, another group of people understood the potential of the sea and the geography of the islands. These were the pirates of the Caribbean: they understood how the shallow waters and numerous reefs could be put to very profitable use.

The Spanish used the Bahamas as a jump-off point for Europe. It was ironic that their ships, laden with treasure which they had plundered from South and Central America, would in turn fall prey to the pirates on their way home. As they made their way sluggishly and carefully through the shallow waters of the Bahamas, they were easy pickings for the pirates, who not only knew the waters like the backs of their hands but also every hiding place from which they could pounce on the treasure ships, and every cave where the treasure could be buried. Names like Captain Kidd, Henry Morgan, William Catt and Anne Bonney are now firmly etched in Caribbean history and there is a strong possibility that somewhere in the Bahamas a massive treasure trove is still waiting to be discovered.

The 'rule' of the pirates continued until the 1700s when, in another of the ironies of Bahamian history, the British appointed an ex-privateer (a type of legal pirate) as the country's first governor. He soon had all the big names in the pirate world captured and hanged, thus ending another chapter in the history of the Bahamas.

The close relationship of the Bahamas and the United States has developed steadily over the centuries. During the Prohibition years, several Bahamians provided a valuable service to many Americans by smuggling rum into the US. Today the well organised tourist industry provides a paradise for these Americans to enjoy, if only for a short time.

Interesting facts about the Bahamas

- During the Second World War, the Governor of the Bahamas was none other than the Duke of Windsor formerly King Edward VIII, who abdicated his throne for the love of a beautiful American woman – Wallis Warfield Simpson.
- The reefs of the Bahamas represent more than 5 per cent of the Earth's total reef mass.

CONCH FRITTERS

In the Bahamas, Cayman and Belize, conch is an integral part of the cuisine. These fritters can be found on many restaurant menus as well as in the most humble homes.

INGREDIENTS

1 lb conch *cleaned*

2 limes

2 tsp salt

2 onions *minced*

6 cloves garlic *minced*

½ oz green onions *minced*

¼ oz fresh parsley *minced*

1 tsp hot pepper sauce

seasoned salt *to taste*

¼ tsp basil

¼ tsp thyme

1½ lb flour

2 tsp baking powder

water

vegetable oil *for frying*

Serves 8

METHOD

Rub the conch with lime and salt and leave it to stand for 5 minutes.

Rinse, then beat the conch with a meat mallet until it is between ½–¼ inch thick. Boil it in salted water for 20 minutes, then drain and rinse. Cut the conch into chunks and process in a food processor for 30 seconds.

Mix all of the remaining ingredients (except the oil) together with the minced conch in a medium-sized bowl and add enough water to make a batter of dropping consistency.

Drop by the spoonful into hot oil and fry until golden.

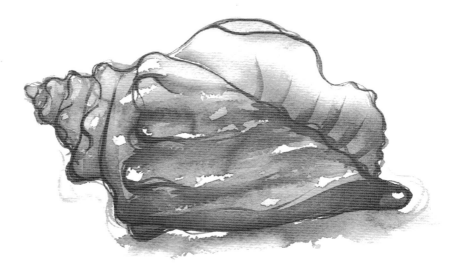

CRACKED CONCH

Whenever I hear the word 'conch' my first thoughts are of the Bahamas and Belize. To the people of those places, this is a very special delicacy.

INGREDIENTS

2 whole conchs *cut in half*

¼ cup lime juice

1 tsp salt

seasoned salt *to taste*

1 cup breadcrumbs ⎫

1 cup flour ⎪

1 tbs granulated garlic ⎬ *for the Breading*

1 tsp salt ⎪

1 tsp paprika ⎭

1 egg *beaten*

oil *for frying*

Serves 4

METHOD

Wash and clean the conch. Beat it with a meat mallet until the sinews are shredded and it flattens to between ¼ – ½ inch thick.

Rub the salt and lime juice into the conch and leave to marinate for 15 minutes.

Rinse, then rub with the seasoned salt.

To make the breading, mix together the flour, breadcrumbs, salt, granulated garlic and paprika.

Dip the conch in the beaten egg then in the breading and sauté quickly in hot oil on each side. Do not overcook because the conch will become rubbery and hard.

Serve with fresh lime, pepper sauce and french fries.

CRAB BACKS

Land crab should be used in this recipe since the flavour when using sea crab is completely different.

In Guyana crabs are caught at night by placing a bright lantern on the ground 'mud flats' where the crabs live. The light attracts them and they come out of their holes and walk towards it. Some 'brave' catchers wear 2 or 3 socks on their hands and actually shove them into the holes in search of the crabs!

INGREDIENTS

1 lb cooked flaked crab meat

2 oz butter

2 green onions *chopped*

1 large onion *chopped*

7 cloves garlic *minced*

salt *to taste*

1 tsp hot pepper sauce

4 tbs Worcestershire sauce

juice of 1 fresh lime

1 cup breadcrumbs

12 crab backs *scrubbed clean or*
    12 foil potato shells

parsley and red bell peppers *for*
    garnish

Serves 12 (makes 20 small shells)

METHOD

Stir-fry the green onions, garlic and onion in butter for 3 minutes. Add the flaked crab meat, Worcestershire sauce, pepper sauce and salt. Add the lime juice.

Cook for about 2 minutes then add the breadcrumbs. Continue to cook for a further 5 minutes. Adjust seasonings to taste.

Spoon the mixture into the crab backs or foil potato shells and dot with butter.

Brown in a hot oven (preheated to 400 °F) for 8 minutes. Garnish with parsley and small pieces of red bell pepper.

Crab Backs

PIRATES OF THE CARIBBEAN

If you were alive back in the seventeenth century and you wanted to become a sailor as a career, you really didn't have a very difficult decision to make. On the one hand, you could join the navy and sail on ships which were captained by people who, on many occasions, had no other qualifications than that they were of the ruling class and who were prone to mistreat their crew. On the other hand, you could become a full blooded Caribbean pirate and sail on ships where even the captain was chosen by a vote and where the 'Articles', like the Ten Commandments, defined strict codes of behaviour for both officers and crew. As a matter of fact, except in times of battle, the captain actually shared his power with the quartermaster who was also responsible for dividing any booty among the crew. Those of you who think that 'Profit Sharing' is a modern concept need to be told that every crew member on a pirate ship was entitled to share in the booty – now if that isn't profit sharing, what is?

Once you signed up for this exciting career, it wouldn't be long before you were bound for the Caribbean, the playground of the pirates. You could be a Buccaneer (the name by which the Caribbean pirates were known) or a Privateer, the difference being that a Buccaneer was free to attack any ship while a Privateer sailed under orders from a government or a large company, although a Privateer too inevitably would 'do his own thing' on occasion. You would feel the excitement as your captain hoisted the Jolly Roger which meant for certain that your ship was about to be involved in a vicious sea battle in which no quarter would be given. Depending on the flamboyance of your captain, this flag – or jack as it was called – would either have been the standard Jolly Roger (skull and crossbones) or one of his own design.

It is easy to see why the Caribbean islands with their several islands and hidden coves provided the perfect location for attacking Spanish treasure ships. The vast treasures that the Spanish were acquiring, at the expense of the original inhabitants of South and Central America and the Caribbean, had to be transported to Spain in slow-moving treasure ships that were perfect prey for the pirates, who would board them and, after the usual energetic battles, relieve them of their treasure. The fact that Spain and England were at each other's throats for most of the period, meant that piracy in one form or another was actually encouraged by the British government who often received a share of any treasure which was acquired.

A few of the pirates went on to bigger things, notably Sir Henry Morgan who was first imprisoned, then knighted for sacking Panama (he later became Governor of Jamaica), and Woodes Rogers who, in his capacity as Governor of the Bahamas, effectively put an end to piracy. Most of their careers didn't have the happy endings that you would expect. . . the notorious 'Blackbeard' was beheaded in a battle with British forces while 'Captain Kidd' was hanged in England.

Piracy was not confined to the men either – two famous pirates, Anne Bonney and Mary Read, were known to be fearless fighters who would fight with any man during their attacks on the treasure ships. They were such fearsome fighters that most of the crew did not even realise that they were women. Both of these ladies sailed with Calico Jack and both were captured when his ship was attacked by the British Navy. They were sentenced to hang but Mary Read had the last laugh when she died from fever while still in jail. Anne Bonney disappeared from all records and it is believed that she was smuggled back to the Carolinas by her rich father.

The legend of the pirates still lives on. Somewhere out there, vast amounts of pirates' treasure is still waiting to be found. . .

CRAB AND DUMPLINGS IN COCONUT SAUCE

Crabs in Coconut Sauce

The people of Trinidad and Dominica make this dish very often. As long as the crabs are 'running' it is sure to be found on the dinner table in many homes.

In the Cayman Islands they make a very similar dish called 'stewed conch'. Instead of crabs, the conch is tenderised with a meat mallet, then boiled in salted water with a squeeze of lemon juice for 15 minutes. It is then cut into bite-sized pieces and stewed with dumplings in the base sauce of the following recipe.

INGREDIENTS

8 whole crabs *backs removed, washed and cleaned*

3 cups water

seasoned salt *to taste*

2 cups coconut milk

6 cloves garlic *sliced*

2 onions *chopped*

½ oz fresh thyme

½ oz fresh marjoram

¼ tsp curry powder

2 stalks celery *diced*

4 tbs parsley *chopped*

½ tsp hot pepper sauce

Dumplings

2 cups flour

¼ tsp salt

1 tbs butter

water

Serves 4

METHOD

Break the crabs in half and place them in a saucepan with the water and seasoned salt. Tie the thyme and marjoram together, place in the water and boil for 10 minutes. Add the coconut milk, dumplings (see recipe below), onions, garlic, celery, parsley, pepper sauce and curry powder.

Simmer for 20 minutes, or until most of the water has evaporated.

The stew can be thickened by mixing a little flour and water together and adding to the gravy.

Serve over boiled rice or breadfruit.

Dumplings

To make the dumplings mix the flour, salt and butter together with enough water to make a stiff dough. Knead it on a floured board for 2 minutes then transfer to a greased bowl, cover with a damp cloth and leave to stand for 5–10 minutes.

Shape the dumplings into balls about 1½ inches in diameter, then press them flat with the palm of your hand.

CEVICHE (MARINATED FISH)

Raw fish is 'cooked' in the very acid lime juice. This delicacy comes from the Maya Indians of Belize. My husband fell in love with it many years ago when my friend Zen, who is from the Philippines, made it for us. It is also one of their national treasures! Isn't it truly amazing how food travels around? The Philippine Islands are very Spanish in many ways and this is also reflected in their cuisine.

INGREDIENTS

1½ lb firm boneless whitefish

1 large onion *cut in julienne strips*

1 red bell pepper *cut in julienne strips*

½ cup chopped cilantro leaves (coriander)

1 cup fresh lime juice

½ Scotch bonnet *or* habanero pepper *chopped*

1 tsp salt

½ tsp MSG (optional)

Serves 4

METHOD

Wash and clean the fish, then cut it into ½ inch cubes.

In a bowl, combine all of the ingredients and mix well.

Refrigerate for at least 2 hours before serving.

The fish will become opaque.

Ceviche

WAYSIDE WORKS

Wherever you go in the Caribbean you are sure to meet the enterprising people who daily contribute to the wayside works. These are the several vendors who use their ingenuity to sell everything from aphrodisiacs to clothing so that they too can enjoy their Caribbean dream.

On your way you'll meet the traditional nutseller, with her packed tray or basket skilfully balanced on her head as she walks the streets offering a selection of fruits, nuts, and other goodies too numerous to mention. She usually beckons you with 'look ma hay' (here I am) and then proceeds to offer you the sweetest mangoes or the freshest roasted peanuts, or whatever other superlative item is up for sale on that day.

A little further along your journey and you're sure to need the services of the coconut vendor, be it the mobile type with carts brimming over with coconuts, or the big wheelers with what seem like miles of coconuts in all shades of green and brown or even bright yellow, packed along the road. These guys use extremely sharp cutlasses or machetes to take the tops off the coconuts and get to the water. I am always amazed that they still have fingers and hands since they never seem to pay attention to what they are doing – well not enough attention when you consider how sharp the cutlasses have to be. If you decide to buy a coconut, the vendor can advise you as to whether it will 'have plenty water' or 'plenty jelly', whether it will be sweet or have a more natural taste. . . whatever you desire. If you are not used to drinking coconuts from the shell, ask for a straw – you'll feel refreshed anyway, whether you drink it or get bathed in it. And while on the subject, be sure to use coconut water as a mixer with your favourite drink. Even sodas which we call soft drinks to differentiate them from hard drinks (liquor) can benefit from a mix with coconut water.

Did I mention soft drinks? Well, if you prefer, you can get your soft drink straight from the refrigerator. Not a plugged-in one but a disused refrigerator from which the compressor and other 'useless' items are removed. It is then fitted with wheels and filled with ice and 'soft drinks'. So now you can tell your friends that you got a cool drink straight from the refrigerator on the corner of a street in town.

Most of the vendors come out at night – the roti vendors in Trinidad, the fish-fryers in Barbados, the barbecuers of whatever calling: all take the sensible option of lighting up their hot fires after the sun goes down.

Two of my favourites are the vendors who sell oysters and conch, both reputed aphrodisiacs. The lambi (conch) vendors in St Lucia come out on Friday nights in Gros Islet, while the oyster salesmen in Trinidad who serve their oysters in the raw can be found around Queens Park Savannah at weekends. These oysters are served with pepper sauce which is either hot, hotter or meltdown – it might just be all that hot pepper and not the oysters that causes those stirrings for which the oysters are given credit. In case you are not used to oysters just remember this: WHATEVER YOU DO – DON'T CHEW!

Egg Balls and Cook-up Rice in Guyana

On your way home from a party in Guyana, typically 2 or 3 o'clock in the morning, the tradition is to visit the wayside vendor to buy a bowl or so of cook-up rice along with some coconut water and steel drops. That's the way to end off a good night's partying. Now you must be wondering what steel drops are. . . well, when I was growing up I used to ask that same question. . . and to this day I am yet to get the same answer twice. All I know is that it is an aphrodisiac and the fellas used to swear that it would put 'lead in your pencil' – if you had a pencil that is. As for the bowl or the bowl and a half – the vendor usually has a bowl, about the size of a cereal bowl, that he uses to dispense the rice in measured quantities.

To enjoy the wayside works anywhere in the Caribbean you first have to know when and where to find them. For example, it would be to your advantage to know that the vendors of egg-balls in Guyana operate mainly outside the cinemas at half-time (intermission). The egg-balls (also called egg-in-ambush) are made from eggs which are first boiled and then encased in a seasoned potato or cassava (yucca) coating to create a delicious golden-brown snack. I haven't yet quite figured out if the 'ambush' refers to the effect that the combination has on some people: it is best to keep out of confined areas for a while after you've eaten a few egg-balls.

Rotis and Doubles in Trinidad

It is the weekend in Trinidad, and St James, one of the more popular hangouts in the country, is buzzing with action. Here, you can find several street vendors selling rotis hot off the tawa. . . for those of you who don't know what a tawa is, it is a round flat piece of iron that you bake the rotis on. My favourite vendor has her dough set out in little mounds on a table together with her pots full of beef, chicken and goat curry, also curried potato, channa and pumpkin – so you can get anything from a totally vegetarian roti to an all meat one. As you will remember from page 52 a roti is very much like a flour tortilla made on a hot griddle. In Trinidad, when it is finished cooking it is beaten with a stick to break it up. The result, which resembles an old shirt that has been torn to shreds, is called 'buss-up shut'. In Guyana it also carries a similarly descriptive name – 'fling up and clap', because it is tossed into the air and clapped about four times once it is cooked. Doing this makes the roti soft and flaky and much nicer for dipping into curries. Another way to eat a roti is to place the curry in the centre and roll it in a similar way to a burrito. Anyway, after a good roti all that remains to be done is wash it down with a cold beer.

One thing you should know though is that, depending on where you are in the Caribbean, purchasing a roti can give you very different results. In many islands, roti means both the meat and the 'flat bread' (skin) but this is not the case in Guyana. If you want a complete roti there, you need to order a roti and curry.

Trinidad is just as famous for its 'doubles' and of course you never make the mistake of ordering one 'double' – the correct order is 'one doubles'. Doubles are another type of flat bread that is fried (bara), filled with curry channa (garbanzoes or chick peas) and bathed in a sauce. It is then wrapped in waxed paper and handed to the customer. The secret to a successful 'doubles' operation, lies not only in the sauce prepared by the vendor (many are tamarind-based with lots of pepper) but in the flair with which they are presented for sale. You can always tell who is the best vendor in both areas by checking the length of the queue waiting to be served.

Mannish Water and Jerk in Jamaica

Mannish water is a soup made with the throw-away bits of the goat, like the head, liver, feet and such like. It is another one of those Caribbean foods that the men believe will put 'lead in your pencil'. The wayside vendors set up shop at the side of the road with their huge cauldrons and dispense the soup into disposable hot cups. Of course there are lots of other ingredients and, unlike other soups, this one is 'eaten' with a fork. Jamaica is also famous for its Jerk Chicken and Jerk Pork, which is made by smoking highly-seasoned chicken or pork over a pimento wood fire in an old oil drum.

Flying Fish and Barbecued Tails in Barbados

In Barbados the vendors set up coalpots at the side of the road to fry fish and chicken and roast corn. Recently they introduced Bar-B-Q pig-tails and that was really a treat. They were so popular that one night I counted about 25 vendors in approximately five miles.

The latest addition to wayside food is in a fishing town called Oistins. The fish market is right on the beach and alongside the market they have built a really nice outdoor area where vendors set up their coal-pots and fry fish straight off the boats. There are picnic tables, music and lots of drinks and the 'lime' goes on on Friday and Saturday nights until sun-up. This is not just the place to visit after leaving a party – many visitors and locals alike make it the venue of their main night out. It's a great place for socialising because you run into so many people you know during the course of the night.

Boiled Corn and Roasted Breadfruit in St Vincent

If you felt like preparing a meal with a roasted breadfruit in Barbados or many of the other islands, you would have to buy a breadfruit and then take it home to roast. In St Vincent however, this is one of the offerings available from the street vendors. They have made cooking breadfruit a science, and so, after carefully selecting a roasting breadfruit as opposed to a boiling breadfruit, they put it on the fire, ready for you to take home and add to your meal.

Another wayside speciality in St Vincent is Boiled Corn which is made from corn boiled in a Callaloo Soup. Once it is cooked, the corn and soup are allowed to cool and then sold to the public in plastic bags. The ear of corn is placed in the bag followed by a ladle of soup. The top of the bag is tied and away you go!

DUCKANOO WITH SALTFISH AND EGGPLANT

INGREDIENTS

Duckanoo

1 lb sweet potatoes *grated raw*

1 lb fresh grated coconut *or* 12 oz desiccated

½ tsp ground cinnamon

½ tsp ground nutmeg

8 oz flour

8 oz sugar

½ cup raisins

2 cups coconut milk

1 tbs almond essence

8 oz margarine *melted*

About 15 eight-inch squares of young banana leaves *or* corn shucks

Saltfish

8 oz boneless salted cod

1 large onion *chopped*

6 cloves garlic *minced*

1 green onion *chopped*

1 red bell pepper *chopped*

2 tomatoes *chopped*

½ tsp thyme

1 tsp hot pepper sauce

seasoned salt *to taste*

1 tsp tomato paste

1 cup water

3 tbs vegetable oil

Eggplant

1 large eggplant

4 cloves garlic *minced*

1 tbs olive oil

salt *to taste*

¼ tsp hot pepper sauce

Serves 6

This is the national dish of Antigua. Although the Duckanoo is similar to the version from Jamaica and Conkies from Barbados, in this instance it is served as part of the main menu. Good Friday has always been regarded as a 'fish day' in many islands of the Caribbean so it is only natural that Antiguans make their national dish on this day.

METHOD

Pass the banana leaves over an open flame on both sides and wipe with a damp cloth. The leaves can also be soaked in boiling water for 2 minutes, then wiped dry.

Mix the flour, sweet potato, coconut, raisins, spices and sugar together, then pour in the essence, coconut milk and melted margarine and mix to a paste of dropping consistency.

Place two tablespoons of the mixture in the centre of the leaf and fold to make a packet. Tie with cord.

Steam on a rack over boiling water for 1 hour, or until firm.

Saltfish

Boil the fish for 5 minutes, drain and cool under running water. Flake the fish and set aside.

Heat the oil and sauté the onion, garlic and green onion for 2 minutes. Add the tomatoes and bell pepper and continue to cook for a further 2 minutes. Stir in the remaining ingredients and simmer for 10 minutes.

Eggplant

Peel the eggplant and cut into quarters. Place in a pan with salted water and boil for 10 minutes, or until tender. Drain and mash with a fork.

Mix in the garlic, oil, salt and pepper sauce.

Note:

The traditional way to serve this dish is to unwrap the Duckanoo and place it on a plate together with the saltfish and eggplant. A piece of boiled ripe plantain is also served as a side dish.

ESCOVEITCHED-COWECHE FISH

This is the Jamaican, Virgin Island and Caymanian version of 'Pescado en Escabeche' found in the Spanish islands. In the Virgin Islands it is known as 'Coweche' and was the dish of choice for taking on long journeys because it was pickled.

INGREDIENTS

3 lb fish fillets

2 eggs *beaten*

4 tsp black pepper

4 tsp salt

2 cups flour

vegetable oil *for frying*

1 tsp hot pepper sauce

1 cup vinegar

1 cup water

1½ tbs sugar

¼ tsp salt

1 tsp ground allspice

3 large onions *sliced*

1 cup christophene, red bell pepper
     and carrots *cut in julienne strips*

Serves 8

METHOD

Mix together the flour, salt and black pepper.

Wash and dry the fish and cut it into 2 oz slices. Dip the fish in the egg, then in the seasoned flour.

Heat oil in a frying pan and fry the fish until crisp on both sides. Set aside in a dish.

Bring to the boil the vinegar, water, sliced onions, allspice, pepper sauce, sugar and salt. Add the vegetables and simmer for 8 minutes. Finally pour it over the fish and leave to steep for at least 1 hour before serving.

Escoveitched Fish

THE VIRGIN ISLANDS

The Virgin Islands, which lie to the east of Puerto Rico, were discovered by Christopher Columbus on his second voyage to the New World, in 1493. The unspoilt beauty of the seven main islands and the more than ninety islets and cays, reminded him of St Ursula's 11,000 virgin followers – hence their name.

Inevitably, the obvious lack of precious metals meant that the Spaniards soon lost interest but the sheer number of tiny islands with their reefs and hidden coves made them a perfect location for the many pirates who plied their trade in the waters of the Caribbean.

The island became home to many now famous pirates – Sir Francis Drake, Blackbeard and Bluebeard – to name but a few.

In 1666 the Danes occupied St Thomas while the British occupied what is now known as the British Virgin Islands which included Tortola and Virgin Gorda. The Danes later occupied St John and finally acquired St Croix from the French in 1733. The US realised the strategic location of the islands with regards to the Panama Canal and purchased St Thomas, St John and St Croix from the Danes in 1917.

The town of Charlotte Amalie which is located on the island of St Thomas, is the capital of the US Virgin Islands while Road Town, located on Tortola, is the capital of the British Virgin Islands.

The pirates have long since been replaced by seafarers of another kind – the thousands of tourists who visit the islands every year to have fun in the sun.

Interesting fact about the Virgin Islands

• Camille Pissarro, a founder and leader of French impressionist art, was born in St Thomas in 1830.

KALALOO

This dish comes from the Virgin Islands and is made with a meat and fish stock. It is served over Plain Fungi on Old Year's Night and is supposed to bring luck in the New Year to all who partake.

INGREDIENTS

12 oz salt pork

12 oz fish fillets *fried the day before*

2 pints water

½ tsp hot pepper sauce

2 lb spinach *coarsely chopped*

1 lb okras *cut in cartwheels*

1 large eggplant *peeled and diced*

1 small can sardines

Serves 4

METHOD

Soak the salt pork in hot water overnight. Wash and drain, then cut into bite-sized pieces. Place the pork and water in a saucepan and bring to the boil. Reduce the heat and simmer for 30 minutes.

In the meantime, flake the cooked fish and set aside.

Remove the pork from the stock after 30 minutes and also set aside.

Steam the spinach and eggplant in the pork stock for 10 minutes, then add the okras and pepper sauce. Simmer for a further 10 minutes, uncovered, as this allows the vegetables to retain their nice green colour.

Return the fish, sardines and meat to the pan, mix and simmer for a final 20 minutes.

Serve over Plain Fungi (see Coo-Coo recipe page 134).

SWEET & SOUR FISH

The islands with a large Asian community are very partial to this dish.

INGREDIENTS

2 lb fish fillets *cut into 4 oz pieces*

salt *to taste*

black pepper *to taste*

1 tbs chopped parsley

1 green onion *chopped*

Batter

1 cup flour

1 pint water

1 tbs baking powder

salt and black pepper *to taste*

vegetable oil *for frying*

Sauce

2 tbs vegetable oil

1 onion *sliced*

1 medium carrot *sliced*

1 green pepper *sliced*

2 tomatoes *sliced*

½ cup tomato ketchup

½ cup sugar

½ cup vinegar

½ cup water

salt *to taste*

1 tbs cornstarch *dissolved in a little water*

Serves 6

METHOD

Clean the fish and season it with salt, black pepper, parsley and green onion; then set aside.

Next, make the sauce by heating the oil and sautéing the onion, carrot, green pepper and tomatoes for 4 minutes. Add the ketchup, sugar, vinegar, water and salt and simmer for a further 15 minutes.

Stir the cornstarch mixture and add to the sauce. Stir until the sauce bubbles and thickens.

Make the batter by mixing the water, baking powder, flour, salt and pepper. Coat the fish and deep fry until crispy.

Place the fish in a serving dish and pour sauce over before serving.

Sweet & Sour Fish garnished with lettuce leaves, lemon, parsley and red pepper

FISH PIE

A fish lover's delight! The flavours of the two types of fish and sweet potatoes come together in a very special way. Even if you are not a 'fish fanatic' this one is sure to please.

INGREDIENTS

4 tbs butter
1 large onion *minced*
3 cloves garlic *minced*
1 lb white fish fillets
1 tsp salt
2 limes
½ lb salted cod fish
1½ lb sweet potatoes *do not peel*
seasoned salt *to taste*
¼ cup milk
3 tbs breadcrumbs
½ tsp hot pepper sauce

Sauce
2 tbs butter
2 tbs flour
salt *to taste*
1¼ cups milk
1 cup cheddar cheese *grated*
1 tsp curry powder
2 tbs parsley *minced*

Serves 4

METHOD

Rub the fish fillets with salt and the juice from the two limes. Set aside for 15 minutes.

In the meantime, boil the saltfish for 5 minutes, then drain and cool under running water. Flake the fish, discarding bones and skin.

Rinse the lime and salt off the fish fillets and pat dry with paper towels.

Sauté the onion and garlic in 2 tablespoons butter for 3 minutes, then add the fish fillets and the saltfish. Add seasoned salt and pepper sauce. Cook for 10 minutes. Stir frequently to break up the fish fillets.

Transfer to an oven-proof dish and set aside.

Boil the sweet potatoes in salted water until tender, then drain and cool. Peel and mash potatoes with the milk and remaining butter. Season to taste.

Sauce
Make the sauce by melting the butter in a pan, then sprinkle over the flour and stir. Add the milk slowly, stirring constantly to break up any lumps. Simmer for 1 minute then add the cheese, curry powder, salt and parsley. Continue to cook until the sauce thickens. This will take about 3 minutes.

Pour the sauce over the fish and mix well. Top with the mashed sweet potato, dot with butter and sprinkle over breadcrumbs. Bake in the oven, preheated to 350 °F, for 30 minutes, or until the top is brown.

FRIZZLED SALTFISH

The Portuguese community in Guyana serve this for breakfast or lunch. It is also a great accompaniment to cocktails! In St Vincent it is served with roasted breadfruit that can be bought ready roasted at the street corners. It's a very fast and simple meal.

INGREDIENTS

8 oz salted cod fish

4 slices bacon *minced*

6 tbs butter

1 large onion *minced*

5 cloves garlic *minced*

3 green onions *chopped*

2 tomatoes *chopped*

1 cucumber *diced*

1 sweet red pepper *seeded and minced*

½ tsp basil

½ tsp thyme

½ tsp hot pepper sauce

Serves 4

METHOD

Boil the saltfish in water for 5 minutes then drain. Cool under running water, then flake, discarding bones and skin.

Sauté the onion and garlic in the butter for 2 minutes, then add the bacon and fish, cover the saucepan and continue cooking for another 2 minutes. Stir in half the green onions, tomatoes, cucumber, sweet pepper, basil, thyme and pepper sauce and simmer for 10 minutes. Add about ½ cup water if it dries out while simmering.

Garnish with the remaining chopped green onion and serve immediately with Roasted Breadfruit (see page 155), boiled rice or crackers.

SANCHOU – SALTFISH AND BREADFRUIT

In Dominica the people also have a passion for breadfruit and saltfish. However, the way it is prepared is quite different from the one that is popular in St Vincent and I thought it would be nice to feature both versions.

INGREDIENTS

8 oz saltfish

1 cup coconut milk

½ cup water

8 cloves garlic *minced*

1 large onion *chopped*

2 stalks celery *diced*

2 tbs chopped parsley

¼ tsp hot pepper sauce

¼ tsp mixed herbs (marjoram, thyme, basil)

4 tbs butter

seasoned salt *to taste*

2 christophenes *boiled in salted water and mashed*

Serves 4

METHOD

Boil the saltfish for 5 minutes, then cool under running water. Flake the fish, discarding any skin and bones.

Heat the butter in a pan and sauté the onion and garlic for 2 minutes; add the parsley and celery. Cook for another 3 minutes, then add the fish and coconut milk, water, herbs, pepper sauce and seasoned salt. Simmer for 5 minutes. Finally, stir in the mashed christophene and heat through.

Serve with boiled or Roasted Breadfruit (see page 155). It is also quite delicious with boiled rice.

GREEN FIG (BANANA) SALAD

St Lucia is a large banana grower and therefore the fruit features prominently in their cuisine. Here is an example of how a fruit can be made into a tasty dish . . . enjoy!

INGREDIENTS

6 green bananas *peeled and boiled in salted water*

3 carrots *boiled in salted water*

3 cloves garlic *minced*

1 small onion *diced*

1 red bell pepper *seeds removed and diced*

4 oz saltfish

1 oz fresh parsley *minced*

¼ tsp habanero *or* Scotch bonnet pepper *minced*

½ cup mayonnaise

Serves 4

METHOD

Boil the saltfish for 5 minutes. Drain and cool under running water then shred, discarding any bones and skin.

In a large bowl, dice the green bananas and carrots. Add the remaining ingredients, including the shredded saltfish, and toss with the mayonnaise.

Marinate in the refrigerator for at least 1 hour before serving.

GUYANA

Guyana is the only English speaking country in South America. Much of the coastline is below sea level but, thanks to the Dutch who settled there in 1615, a massive wall (sea wall) and a series of dams and groynes were constructed to protect the rich fertile coastline from incursion by the sea. Originally called British Guiana after it became a British colony in 1831, Guyana, as it was renamed after independence in 1966, boasts a rich cultural heritage which includes not only that of its original Amerindian inhabitants but also Dutch, British, African, Chinese, Portuguese and East Indian races.

The Dutch themselves may be long gone, but everywhere you go, Dutch names remind you of their 200-year presence in Guyana. Prior to the English colonisation, the capital Georgetown was known as Stabroek and today Stabroek market continues to play a major role in the life of the Guyanese people. A visit there is sure to open your eyes to the multicultural nature of Guyana's people as they animatedly negotiate with the vendors for the exotic fruit and other offerings which are on sale. However no visit to Guyana is complete without a trip to what all Guyanese know as 'the interior'.

From my experience, the interior for most Guyanese starts just outside the city limits, as the little pockets of civilisation become fewer and fewer and the trees take over.

From the coastline, which is below sea level, a journey inland can take you anywhere from the vast Rupununi savannah to mountains, forests, massive rivers or quaint Amerindian villages. You can experience the Kaieteur Falls, which are five times the height of the Niagara Falls but in a totally natural setting, or swim in creeks where the water is so black that if you take a photograph in broad daylight it triggers your flash. If you are lucky (depending on your point of view) you may get a chance to see anything from beautiful birds, to black crocodiles (caiman) to wild pigs, all of which contribute to Guyana's attraction as a holiday destination.

Interesting facts about Guyana

- Kaieteur Falls, with a single drop of over 700 feet, is the largest single-drop falls in the world. In total it drops over 800 feet making it five times the height of Niagara Falls.
- Guyana is home to the Arapaima – the largest freshwater fish in the world.
- Over 700 indigenous species of birds live in Guyana's forests.
- St George's Cathedral in Georgetown is one of the tallest wooden buildings in the world.

INGREDIENTS

2 lb fish fillets

¼ cup lime juice

2 tbs salt

1 lb sweet potatoes *peeled and sliced 1½ inches thick*

1 lb white potatoes *peeled*

1 lb yams (tarro) *peeled and sliced 1½ inches thick*

1 lb eddoes *peeled*

1 breadfruit *peeled, heart removed and cut into eights*

(turnips may be used if any of the above are not available)

4 onions *peeled*

½ lb okras

1 head cabbage *cut in quarters with heart removed*

1 lb carrots *peeled and cut in half*

3 cups coconut milk

salt *to taste*

1 oz fresh thyme

1 oz fresh marjoram

1 whole Scotch bonnet *or* habanero pepper

4 oz salt pork

Seasoning

3 cloves garlic

1 green onion

½ onion

1 tsp thyme

1 tsp marjoram

¼ tsp salt

habanero *or* Scotch bonnet pepper *to taste*

1 tbs Worcestershire sauce

¼ tsp ground cloves

4 tbs white vinegar

Serves 8

METAGEE

The African slaves ate ground provisions as a major part of their diet. This recipe is popular to this day in many islands. In Guyana it is known as Metagee, in St Lucia as Oil Down, in Jamaica and Cayman as Rundown and in Barbados, Stew Food. Although the basic recipe varies slightly in each island the common thread is clear.

METHOD

Place all the ingredients for the seasoning into a blender and process for about 30 seconds.

Rub the fish with salt and lime juice and set aside for 15 minutes.

Rinse and pat dry, then score the fish and insert the seasoning into the slits. Rub the entire fillet with the seasoning and adjust salt to taste. Set aside to marinate for 15 minutes.

Place the sweet potatoes, yams, eddoes, white potatoes and breadfruit in a large stockpot.

On top of them place the carrots, cabbage, onions, okras and fish. Make sure that the firm vegetables are on the bottom of the pot and the delicate ones on the top.

Tie the marjoram and thyme together and put into the pot together with the pepper and salt pork.

Season the coconut milk with salt, then pour into the pot. Add enough water to bring the level of the liquid just below the okras and fish.

Bring to the boil and simmer for about 30 minutes or until the vegetables on the bottom are tender and the level of the liquid has dropped by three quarters.

Serve at once.

Note:

Barbadian Seasoning can be substituted for the above (see recipe, page 123).

MAUFFAY

This next recipe hails from the Virgin Islands and the base stock is the same as Kalaloo which is the dish traditionally served on Old Year's Night. Mauffay is a very thick stew (thickened by cornmeal) and served over Plain Fungi. As you may have noticed, in the Caribbean a lot of our food is cooked with salt pork, coconut milk and saltfish. In the old days when money was in short supply and many families were quite large, it was these ingredients that made dinner-time such a tasty affair while allowing a little to go a long way.

INGREDIENTS

8 oz salt pork

1½ lb fish fillets *fried the day before*

6 cups water

1 head celery *diced*

1 oz fresh parsley *chopped*

2 large tomatoes *diced*

6 cloves garlic *minced*

1 large onion *diced*

2 green onions *chopped*

1 tsp hot pepper sauce

2 bay leaves

1 oz fresh thyme

1 oz fresh marjoram

3 tbs cornmeal

1 tbs butter

seasoned salt *to taste*

Serves 8

METHOD

Soak the salt pork in hot water overnight. Wash and drain the meat then place in a saucepan with the water to boil. Cook for 20 minutes, then add the garlic, onion, tomatoes, green onions, celery, parsley, pepper sauce and bay leaves. Tie the marjoram and thyme together with some string and lower into the pot. Continue to simmer for a further 20 minutes.

In the meantime flake the fish and set aside.

After the 20 minutes, stir in the fish and butter. Adjust the taste to your liking with the seasoned salt and simmer for 5 minutes. Mix the cornmeal with ½ cup water and pour slowly into the stew. Cook for a further 7 minutes, then serve hot over Plain Fungi (see page 134).

RED HERRING AND COO-COO

Referred to as 'peasant food' in the old days, this dish provided a cheap source of protein.

INGREDIENTS

2 smoked herrings

1 onion *chopped*

6 cloves garlic *minced*

1 large tomato *diced*

½ tsp basil

½ tsp thyme

¼ tsp hot pepper sauce

3 tbs butter

½ cup water

Serves 4

METHOD

Soak the herring in boiling water for at least 3 hours then drain. Remove the skin and as many of the bones as possible and discard them. Strip the fish into one-inch pieces and set aside.

Heat the butter in a saucepan and add the onion and garlic. Stir-fry until the onion is limp (about 3 minutes), then add the tomato. Continue to stir-fry for another 2 minutes before adding the fish, pepper sauce and herbs. Pour in ¼ cup water, cover and simmer for 5 minutes.

Serve over Coo-Coo (see recipe page 134).

Red Herring and Coo-Coo (garnished with strips of red pepper and a sprig of thyme)

SALTFISH PIE

Salted cod was another cheap source of protein in the days before refrigerators. This type of fish is still widely used in all the Caribbean islands even though the price is now more reflective of a gourmet item.

INGREDIENTS

1 lb boneless salted cod

2 cups milk

3 tbs flour

3 tbs butter

¼ tsp hot pepper sauce

1 lb yams *boiled and sliced ½ inch thick*

1 onion *sliced*

½ cup grated cheese

2 tbs chopped parsley

2 hardboiled eggs *sliced*

2 green onions *chopped*

Serves 4

METHOD

Boil the fish for 5 minutes. Drain and cool under running water. Flake the fish and set aside.

Make a white sauce by melting the butter then adding the flour and milk, stirring continuously to break up any lumps. Stir in the pepper sauce.

In a greased oven-proof dish, arrange a layer of yams, saltfish, onion, eggs, green onions and parsley. Pour over the sauce then repeat layers ending with sauce and grated cheese.

Bake in a preheated oven, 350 °F, until brown.

SALTFISH SOUFFLE

Salted cod is very versatile and this recipe demonstrates that admirably . . .

INGREDIENTS

6 oz boneless salted codfish

2 tbs butter

3 tbs flour

½ cup milk

¼ tsp hot pepper sauce

1 green onion *chopped*

1 tbs parsley *chopped*

1 green onion *chopped*

3 eggs *separated*

Serves 4

METHOD

Boil the saltfish for 5 minutes, then cool under running water. Flake the fish.

Melt the butter in a saucepan, then add the flour and milk, stirring all the time. Bring to the boil, then stir in the saltfish, onion, green onion, parsley and pepper sauce.

Turn off the heat.

Beat the eggs yolks and stir into the mixture. Beat the egg whites until stiff, then fold in.

Pour into a greased oven-proof dish and bake in a preheated oven, 350 °F, until brown and the mixture is set.

STUFFED RED SNAPPER

Fresh seafood reigns supreme in Belize and this dish is made on special occasions there. Share it with someone special – they'll never forget the experience!

INGREDIENTS

2 tbs butter *melted*

2 tbs salt

½ cup lime juice

2 small red snappers – 1½ lb each
     heads removed (optional)

4 slices bacon

2 tbs vegetable oil

seasoned salt *to taste*

1 tsp hot pepper sauce

2 tbs lemon juice

Stuffing

2 tbs butter

1 cup boiled rice

¼ tsp hot pepper sauce

1 onion *minced*

1 cup ham *diced*

1 tsp grated lemon rind

3 tbs cilantro (coriander) *minced*

1 tsp fresh thyme *minced*

1 tsp fresh marjoram *minced*

1 tbs Worcestershire sauce

seasoned salt *to taste*

1 egg *lightly beaten*

1¾ cups breadcrumbs

Serves 4

METHOD

First, make the stuffing. Sauté the onion in 2 tablespoons butter, then add the ham, rice, lemon rind, cilantro, herbs, seasoned salt, Worcestershire sauce and pepper sauce, and cook for 3 minutes. Stir in the breadcrumbs and cook for 2 more minutes. Allow to cool slightly, then mix in the egg.

Next, rub salt and lime juice all over the fish and allow it to stand for 15 minutes. Then rinse it and pat it dry with paper towels.

Now, rub each fish with seasoned salt, pepper sauce and lemon juice, then stuff each one with half of the stuffing. Wrap 2 bacon slices around each fish, place in a greased, oven-proof dish and pour over the melted butter and oil.

Finally, bake in a preheated oven 275 °F for 45 minutes, or until the fish flakes easily when tested with a fork. Baste occasionally during baking.

Stuffed Red Snapper, wrapped in bacon

vegetables and side dishes

AKRA

In the Virgin Islands this fritter is still a special treat. It came from Africa all those years ago when our forefathers were brought to work in the cane fields.

INGREDIENTS

8 oz blackeye peas *soaked overnight*

½ tsp hot pepper sauce

4 okras *cut in cartwheels*

½ cup water

seasoned salt *to taste*

vegetable oil *for frying*

Serves 4

METHOD

Wash and drain the peas, then rub them between your fingers to remove the skins. Grind them in a coffee mill or process to a paste in a food processor.

Mix together the paste, okras, seasoned salt, pepper sauce and water to make a stiff batter.

Drop by the teaspoonful into hot oil and fry until golden brown. Drain on paper towels and serve warm as an appetiser, or when sharing a drink with friends.

TUK BAND

The Tuk Band in Barbados is another example of the blending of cultures that took place in the Caribbean. The 'Tuk Band' usually comprises a bass drum, a kettle or snare drum, a triangle or other percussive instrument and a penny whistle or flute. Characters representing our African heritage of masquerade are often featured. These are the Stiltman, the Donkey, the Shaggy Bear and the Mother Sally.

The word 'Tuk' itself is thought to be derived from the Scottish word 'Touk' meaning to beat or sound an instrument. The drum music of the band is firmly rooted in our African culture and was brought to Barbados with the arrival of the first slaves in 1627, while the Tuk Band itself owes its origins to the fife and drum marching bands of the eighteenth century British regiments. The end result is music with an easily recognisable African base upon which British regimental rhythms and Barbadian experiences have been superimposed.

Tuk Bands exist in many Caribbean islands, where they are known as Masquerade Bands.

BARBADIAN SEASONING

This seasoning is the secret to the success of many mouth-watering Barbadian dishes. It is found in almost every home and comes in several variations. This one is particularly nice.

INGREDIENTS

1½ cups vinegar

2 oz thyme

2 oz parsley

1 lb onions

5 oz green onions

2 oz marjoram

4 Scotch bonnet peppers *or* habanero (add more to make it hotter)

4 oz garlic

½ oz ground clove

2 tbs Worcestershire sauce

¼ tsp black pepper

4½ tbs salt

½ tsp MSG *(optional)*

METHOD

Remove the stems from the thyme and marjoram and place in a blender with the vinegar. Liquefy.

Place the onions, green onions, parsley, peppers and garlic in a food processor and process for 30 seconds to 1 minute. Blend this together with the seasoned vinegar in a mixing bowl.

Stir in the salt, MSG, Worcestershire sauce, ground clove and black pepper. Bottle and refrigerate.

Leave it to stand for one week, before using as required.

Note:
Barbadian Seasoning will keep in the refrigerator for up to 6 months.

BAR-B-Q MARINADE

Use this marinade on your favourite barbecue meats or poultry and you can forget the barbecue sauce. The flavour is totally absorbed by the meat and is released when you bite into it.

INGREDIENTS

2 medium onions *peeled*
1 head garlic *peeled*
4 tbs salt
2 tsp thyme
2 tsp oregano
2 tsp basil
2 tbs sugar
1 cup white vinegar
1 cup orange juice
4 tbs tomato paste
½ Scotch bonnet *or* habanero
    pepper
½ cup rum
2 tbs liquid hickory

METHOD

Place all the ingredients in a blender and purée for about one minute.

Allow the chicken or pork to soak in this marinade for at least 2 hours before grilling.

Note:

This is enough to marinate at least 40 pieces of chicken. Use what you need and freeze the remainder.

BLACK BEANS AND RICE

Whenever black beans and rice is mentioned it is Cuba that comes to mind. However, this dish is also one of the staples in Belize, no doubt because of the Spanish influence.

INGREDIENTS

1½ cups dried black beans *soaked overnight, or* 1 can (16 oz) canned variety

½ lb ham *diced*

2 tbs vegetable oil

1 large onion *minced*

5 cloves garlic *minced*

3 tomatoes *chopped*

1 green pepper *chopped*

2 cups long grain rice *washed and soaked for 2 hours*

seasoned salt *to taste*

1 tsp hot pepper sauce

Serves 6

METHOD

Boil the beans in salted water until tender. Drain and refresh under cold water.

Heat the oil in a pan and sauté the onion, garlic, tomatoes and green pepper for 5 minutes.

Drain the rice and add to the pan together with the beans and ham. Season to taste with seasoned salt and pepper sauce. Pour in enough water to barely cover the mixture and simmer covered until the liquid has evaporated.

Serve with your favourite meat, poultry or fish dish.

(see **Note** on page 33 re cooking peas/beans.)

Black Beans and Rice, garnished with red, green and yellow peppers

BLACKEYE PEAS SALAD

Blackeye peas are an excellent source of protein and are very widely used in our cuisine.

INGREDIENTS

2 cups cooked blackeye peas

8 oz lean smoked pork *or* smoked
    ham

½ cup celery *diced*

½ cup each diced red and green
    bell peppers

1 cup sliced cooked carrots

1 small onion *thinly sliced*

2 tbs chopped parsley

¼ cup wine vinegar

4 tbs Dijon mustard

salt and pepper *to taste*

Serves 4

METHOD

In a large bowl toss together the blackeye peas, pork, celery, peppers, carrots and onion.

Make a dressing by mixing together the parsley, vinegar, mustard, salt and pepper. Pour over the peas and mix well.

Refrigerate for at least 1 hour before serving.

Blackeye Peas Salad

BREADFRUIT AND
CHEESE PUFFS

This is what we call finger food, loved by both children and adults.

INGREDIENTS

1½ lb breadfruit *peeled and boiled*
    in salted water until tender

seasoned salt *to taste*

½ tsp hot pepper sauce

1 tbs butter

¼ cup water

3 tbs flour

2 eggs

4 oz cheddar cheese *grated*

vegetable oil *for frying*

Serves 4

METHOD

Mash the breadfruit and then pass through a potato ricer. Blend in the seasoned salt and pepper sauce.

In a pan, bring the butter and water to the boil, then add the flour and beat over a low fire until the mixture forms a ball. Remove the pan from the heat and beat in the eggs until the mixture becomes elastic. Add the breadfruit and cheese and mix well.

Place the mixture into a forcing bag fitted with a plain tube and pipe ½ inch lengths into hot oil. Fry until golden brown.

BREADFRUIT BALLS

*More finger food: the variety of Caribbean hors d'oeuvres that are
served at cocktail parties is nothing short of wonderful!*

INGREDIENTS

1 ripe breadfruit

2 onions *chopped*

10 cloves garlic *minced*

4 green onions (seasoning)
   chopped

¼ tsp roasted ground geera (cumin)

seasoned salt *to taste*

1 tsp hot pepper sauce

1½ cups all-purpose flour

3 eggs *beaten*

breadcrumbs *for rolling*

vegetable oil *for frying*

Serves 6

METHOD

Peel the breadfruit, cut it into pieces and boil in salted water until
very tender. Place the pieces in a large bowl and mash.

Blend in the onions, garlic, flour, green onions, cumin,
seasoned salt, 1 egg and pepper sauce. The mixture should be firm
and stiff. If it is not, add a little more flour. Allow it to cool, then
shape into balls about 2½ inches in diameter.

Roll the balls in breadcrumbs, then in the remaining beaten
eggs and deep fry in hot oil until golden.

CABBAGE AND BACON SALAD

This salad is still crunchy although the cabbage is cooked. Many years ago my friend Ferdinand Hinds, a Barbadian, made this salad for me, and I fell in love with it at once. I especially like serving it as a side dish when Bar-B-Q chicken or pig-tails are on the grill. Because our weather never varies more than 3 degrees year round that can be anytime!

INGREDIENTS

1 head of cabbage *cut into thin strips with hard spines removed*

8 oz bacon *or* sizzlean *cut into ¼ inch julienne strips*

4 tbs vegetable oil

Dressing

½ cup mayonnaise

½ tsp seasoned salt

¼ tsp hot pepper sauce

¼ tsp paprika

⅛ tsp MSG (optional)

Serves 6

METHOD

Heat 1 tablespoon of oil in a wok and fry the bacon for 3 minutes. Remove it from the pan and drain on paper towel.

Now add the remaining oil and stir-fry the cabbage for about 4 minutes. The cabbage should still be fairly crisp. Place the cabbage together with the bacon in a mixing bowl.

Make the dressing by mixing all of the ingredients together and adjust the seasonings to taste.

Toss the cabbage and bacon with the dressing and refrigerate for at least 2 hours for the flavours to blend.

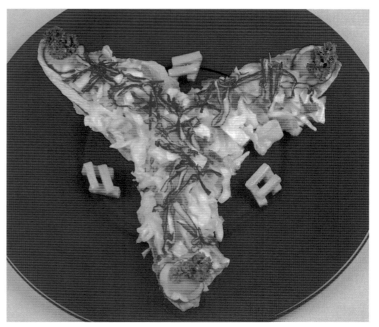

Cabbage and Bacon Salad

CANDIED SWEET POTATOES

At Christmas-time, or anytime that the family gathers, this recipe fits right in.

INGREDIENTS

2½ lb sweet potatoes *scrubbed*

4 tbs brown sugar

¾ cup orange juice

¼ cup rum

¼ cup golden raisins

2 tbs butter

pinch grated nutmeg

Serves 6

METHOD

Boil the sweet potatoes for 20–30 minutes, or until tender. Drain and cool under running water. Peel and slice the potatoes into ¼ inch thick slices.

In a greased oven-proof dish layer the potatoes.

Mix the rum, orange juice, sugar and raisins then pour over the potatoes. Sprinkle on the nutmeg, dot with butter and bake in a preheated oven (350 °F) for 30 minutes.

(See photo, page 56.)

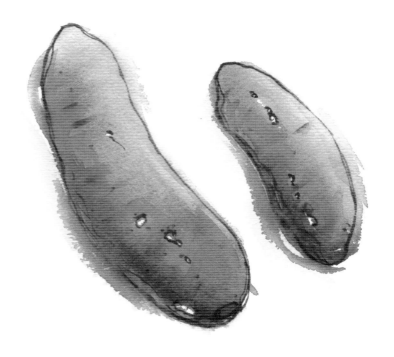

CHRISTOPHENE au GRATIN

Christophenes are also called Chayote and Cho-Cho in some islands. They are light green in colour and shaped like a large pear. In Guadeloupe and Martinique this next recipe is served as a side dish.

INGREDIENTS

4 christophenes

4 tbs breadcrumbs

Sauce

3 tbs butter *or* margarine

3 tbs flour

1¼ cups milk

1 small onion *minced*

pinch grated nutmeg

½ tsp salt

black pepper *to taste*

Serves 4

METHOD

Boil the whole christophenes in salted water for 20 minutes, or until tender. Drain and cool under running water. Peel, quarter and cut out the seeds. Mash with a fork. Squeeze in a cheesecloth to remove excess liquid.

To make the sauce, melt the butter in a saucepan and sprinkle over the flour. Stir, then slowly add the milk. Stirring constantly, add the onion. Season to taste with salt, pepper and the nutmeg. Simmer on low heat for 3 minutes, or until the sauce thickens.

Mix the christophene purée with the sauce, then pour into a greased oven-proof dish and sprinkle with breadcrumbs. Bake in a preheated oven, 350 °F, for 30 minutes or until the top is brown.

COCONUT EGGPLANT

As you can see, coconut milk is used as an integral part of Caribbean cooking. This recipe from St Maarten is a vegetarian's delight.

INGREDIENTS

2 large eggplants
1 tbs salt
vegetable oil *for frying*
3 tbs shredded coconut

Sauce
2 tbs vegetable oil
2 onions *sliced*
4 cloves garlic *minced*
4 tomatoes *peeled and chopped*
1¼ cups coconut milk
seasoned salt *to taste*
1 tsp hot pepper sauce

Serves 4

METHOD

Wash the eggplants and cut into ½ inch thick slices. Sprinkle over the salt and allow to drain for 30 minutes. Rinse under cold water, then pat dry with paper towel. Heat 2 tablespoons of oil in a frying pan and fry the eggplant for 5 minutes, turning once. Add more oil as necessary to fry all the eggplant slices. Drain on paper towel.

To make the sauce heat 2 tablespoons of oil in a pan and sauté the onions, garlic and tomatoes for 5 minutes, stirring constantly. Pour in the coconut milk, seasoned salt and pepper sauce and simmer for 8 minutes.

Layer the eggplant in an oven-proof dish and pour over the sauce. Cover with foil and bake in a preheated oven, 350 °F, for 30 minutes.

Uncover, sprinkle on the shredded coconut and return to the oven for a further 15 minutes.

BARBADOS

Barbados is unique among the Caribbean islands. It is the most easterly of the islands and stands outside of the Caribbean chain. It was never sighted by Christopher Columbus and although it was discovered by a Portuguese navigator Pedro a Campos in 1536, all he did was to give it a name and report his discovery to the Crown. Throughout the years when the European powers were busy colonising the islands, Barbados was left well alone – after all it had no gold or crops that would make anyone a fortune. It was only in 1625 that an English merchant ship on its way from South America landed on Barbados and saw the island's potential for growing tobacco, which was the current 'big money' crop.

Two years later the *William and John* landed on Barbados to establish a colony under the patronage of Sir William Courteen who had been granted all rights to the island by the king of England. The colonists consisted of 80 men and included 10 Africans who were captured from a Portuguese trading vessel. The colonists landed on the island's west coast and named the area Jamestown (now Holetown) after King James, who had by this time died. Two years later the new king, Charles 1, awarded the island to the Earl of Carlisle, who had realised by this time how profitable Barbados was becoming. So now we had two sets of legal owners. The Carlisle colonists settled in St Michael in an area which has through the years developed into the city of Bridgetown.

Since being first settled Barbados remained an English colony, until it became independent on 30 November 1966. It is often referred to as 'Little England' because of its continued English traditions.

Interesting facts about Barbados
- Barbados is the third oldest parliament in the British Commonwealth.
- It is home to one of the oldest Jewish synagogues in the Western hemisphere.
- Barbados is the first producer of rum in the world.
- Barbados is the only country ever to be visited by George Washington.

COO-COO – FUNGI

Coo-Coo and Flying Fish is the national dish of Barbados. In Dominica, Antigua and the Virgin Islands it is know as 'Fungi'. The Italians make a similar dish called 'Polenta'.
Plain Fungi is made by omitting the okras.

INGREDIENTS

15 okras *soaked in 4 cups water*

1 lb cornmeal

6 cups water

1 tsp salt *or to taste*

3 tbs margarine

1 onion *chopped*

5 cloves garlic *minced*

Serves 4

METHOD

Wash the okras and cut off the heads and tails. Cut into cartwheels and place in a pot with 2 cups water and all the other ingredients except the cornmeal. Bring to the boil and simmer for about 15 minutes.

In the meantime, place the cornmeal in a bowl and pour over 4 cups water to saturate the meal. Stir to make sure it is wet throughout.

After the 15 minutes pour out about three quarters of the okras and the cooking liquid and set aside.

Return the pot to a very low heat and pour in the wet cornmeal. Stir constantly to break up any lumps. Add the reserved okras and liquid a little at a time ... stirring to make sure the mixture is smooth. A coo-coo stick is normally used for this purpose – it resembles a small cricket bat. However, a wooden spoon also does the job quite well.

Continue to stir and cook on very low heat for about 10 minutes. When finished the Coo-Coo should be smooth and stiff.

Transfer to a buttered dish.

Serve hot with Steamed Flying Fish or your favourite stew. . .

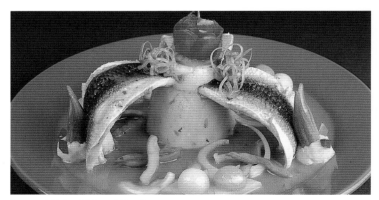

Steamed Flying Fish and Coo-Coo

CHANNA CURRY

When I was a teenager in Guyana, there was a special shop that sold the best tasting Channa. The owner became known as 'Channa Man' and I remember riding my motorcycle late at night or whenever the urge hit me to get some. He disappeared some years ago and resurfaced in Scarborough, Canada, where the tradition continues. The restaurant is called 'Channa Man' and it sells a variety of Caribbean delicacies.

The secret to preparing this dish is using roasted geera (cumin). The flavour is very different.

INGREDIENTS

1 lb channa (chick peas *or* garbanzos)

1 large onion *chopped.*

5 cloves garlic *minced*

salt *to taste*

1 tsp hot pepper sauce

1 tbs ground cumin (roasted)

4 tbs vegetable oil

1 tbs curry powder

3 pints salted water

Serves 6

METHOD

Soak the channa in water overnight. Wash and drain and put into a pressure cooker. Add 3 pints salted water and pressure-cook for 30 minutes. Drain and set aside.

In a wok or large saucepan heat the oil, then stir-fry the onion, and garlic for a few minutes. Add the cumin, curry powder, salt and pepper sauce. Stir twice, then pour in the channa. Adjust seasonings to taste. Continue to stir-fry for a few minutes until the onion is cooked.

Serve over rice or as a side dish.

Note:

The Tamarind Sauce found on page 47 is perfect as a condiment to accompany the channa.

Chicken Curry and Roti with Channa Curry (garnished with strips of red and green pepper)

EGGPLANT CASSEROLE

The Caribbean version of an Italian favourite.

INGREDIENTS

2 large eggplants *sliced ⅛ inch thick*

3 oz ham *chopped*

3 oz cheddar cheese *grated*

2 cups pizza sauce

½ tsp mixed herbs

non-stick cooking spray

Serves 4

METHOD

Mix the herbs with the pizza sauce.

In an oven-proof dish that has been sprayed with non-stick spray, layer the eggplant, pizza sauce, ham and cheese. Repeat to fill dish. Cover with foil and bake for 30 minutes in a preheated oven, 350 °F. Uncover and bake for a further 20 minutes.

EGGPLANT CHOKA

One of my personal favourites, this dish has its roots in India.

INGREDIENTS

1 large eggplant

2 cloves garlic *cut in half*

salt *to taste*

⅛ tsp minced Scotch bonnet *or* habanero pepper

2 tbs vegetable oil

½ tomato *cut into 4 wedges*

1 clove garlic *minced*

¼ onion *minced*

Serves 2

METHOD

Wash and score the eggplant with a knife. Insert the halved garlic and four tomato wedges into the slits. Rub the eggplant with 1 teaspoon oil and roast over an open flame or under the grill of an electric or gas cooker until soft. The open flame (for example, a gas cooker) works the best.

Remove the charred skin and mash the eggplant in a bowl. Add the minced garlic, onion, salt, pepper and the remaining oil.

Serve over hot boiled rice, with Roti or as a side dish.

Note:

The traditional way to roast the eggplant is on an open flame. When it is done this way the taste is much better. Chicken that has been cooked on an outdoor Bar-B-Q grill is superior in flavour to the one done with Bar-B-Q Sauce in the oven. I suppose this is the best way I can explain the difference between the two methods of roasting.

Eggplant Choka, garnished with carrots and okra slices

FANCY POTATO SALAD

For a special occasion, this salad is a treat. It has great eye appeal and also tastes good.

INGREDIENTS

3 cups potatoes *boiled and diced*

1 cup beets *boiled and diced*

1 red bell pepper *diced*

1 cup grapes *halved*

¼ cup walnut pieces

2 hard-boiled eggs *diced*

2 tbs onion *grated* ⎫

salt, pepper and garlic ⎬ *for the*

   powder *to taste* ⎭ *dressing*

½ cup mayonnaise

Serves 6

METHOD

In a bowl, toss the potatoes, beets, bell pepper, grapes, walnuts and eggs.

To make the dressing, mix together the mayonnaise, onion, salt, pepper, and garlic powder.

Combine and chill for 1 hour before serving.

Fancy Potato Salad, garnished with lettuce leaves and grapes

FRIED EGGPLANT

The East Indian influence is very strong in this recipe which is popular in the countries where they settled, for example, Guyana and Trinidad and Tobago.

INGREDIENTS

1 large eggplant

2 cups phulouri batter – see recipe,
    page 147

salt *to taste*

vegetable oil *for frying*

Serves 2

METHOD

Wash and slice the eggplant lengthways. The slices should be around ¼ inch thick. Add ½ cup water to the phulouri batter and salt to taste. Dip the eggplant slices into the batter then fry on both sides until golden.

Serve as a side dish.

HAITI

Two independent and diverse countries share the Caribbean island of Hispaniola: Haiti, which occupies the western third while the Dominican Republic occupies the remainder. Haiti, is the western hemisphere's second oldest independent country (after the United States) and the world's oldest black republic. Two years after the French Revolution in 1789, the slaves in the colony, under the leadership of Toussaint l'Ouverture, rebelled and, in 1791, gained control of the country. However, it was not until 1804, after having defeated a French army under General Charles le Clerc, which was sent to regain the country, that Haiti formally declared its independence. Le Clerc did succeed in capturing Toussaint but the Haitian forces under Jean Jacques Dessalines and Henry Christophe ultimately defeated the French.

Interesting fact about Haiti
- Haiti is the world's oldest black republic and the western hemisphere's second oldest independent country.

GREEN PLANTAIN CHIPS

These are a great substitute for potato fries and are even served for breakfast together with fried eggs and bacon. In Puerto Rico they are called 'Tostones', in Guadeloupe, Martinique and Haiti 'Banane Pese'. They are also a great snack when friends drop by for a drink!

INGREDIENTS

4 green plantains *peeled and sliced into rounds 1½ inch thick*

2 tsp salt

1 tsp Scotch bonnet or habanero pepper *minced*

vegetable oil *for frying*

Serves 2

METHOD

Mix the salt, water and pepper together, then soak the plantain slices in this solution for 30 minutes. Drain and pat dry with paper towel.

Heat some oil in a shallow pan and fry the plantains for 2 minutes. Remove with a slotted spoon and drain. They should be partially cooked and not very crisp. Flatten in a tostones press, or place each slice between waxed paper and flatten with a rolling pin or bottle. Drop them back into the salted water for 10 seconds. Pat dry with paper towel and deep fry until crisp and golden. Drain the excess oil on paper towel.

Serve them immediately.

(See photo on page 39)

JUG JUG

This one is a traditional Barbadian Christmas delicacy and is served as a side dish. It resembles pâté and can also be served as a snack with crackers.

INGREDIENTS

2 cans (16 oz) green pigeon peas

2 oz ham *cubed*

2 oz roast pork

3 onions *sliced*

8 cloves garlic – *cut in half*

1 oz fresh parsley

1 oz salt pork (optional)

¼ habanero *or* Scotch bonnet
    pepper

1 oz fresh basil

1 oz fresh thyme

4 oz guinea corn *or* wholewheat
    flour

Serves 8

METHOD

Drain the peas and place in a saucepan with the ham, pork, salt pork, onions, garlic, parsley and pepper. Tie together the thyme and basil and also place in the pan. Cover with 2 pints water and bring to the boil. Simmer for about 20 minutes, then drain, saving the liquid in a bowl. Remove the thyme and basil and discard.

Process the peas, ham and seasonings in a food processor using a little of the liquid as required. It should have a smooth, stiff consistency.

Mix the flour with 1 cup cold water. In a saucepan bring 1½ cups of the peas' water to the boil and slowly pour in dissolved flour mixture, stirring constantly. Continue to cook on low heat for 5 minutes.

Place the peas' mixture in another saucepan and slowly add the flour stirring with a wooden spoon or coo-coo stick. Add a little of the peas' liquid if necessary but keep it stiff. Cook on a very low heat for about 10 minutes.

Serve as a side dish to accompany roast chicken or turkey.

MACARONI PIE

This is one of the most popular dishes in Barbados. It can be found on many restaurant menus, at weddings, at Christmas time, Sunday lunch or just plain any old day of the week.

INGREDIENTS

1 pack (12 oz) macaroni

½ cup flour

4 tbs butter

1 onion *grated*

¼ cup tomato ketchup

2 cups milk

3 oz grated cheddar cheese

1 cup smoked sausage *diced*
    (optional)

⅛ tsp seasoned salt

1 oz grated cheddar cheese and ⅛
    tsp paprika *for garnish*

Serves 4

METHOD

Prepare the macaroni according to package directions and set aside.

Melt the butter in a pan and add the flour to make a roux. Slowly add the milk, stirring all the time. Add the cheese, ketchup and seasoned salt and cook for about 2 minutes – until the cheese is melted and the sauce is smooth and thick. Use a balloon whisk to make the sauce smooth.

In a large bowl mix together the macaroni, onion, sauce and sausage.

Grease an oven-proof dish and pour in the macaroni mixture. Sprinkle on some grated cheese and paprika then bake in a preheated oven, 350 °F, for 30 minutes.

Serve as a side dish or with your favourite meat, poultry or fish dish.

Macaroni Pie, garnished with carrot balls and green peas

MARINATED CARROTS

These carrots are a nice side dish to accompany any kind of Bar-B-Q.

INGREDIENTS

1 lb carrots *sliced and cooked in salted water*

1 sweet pepper *cut into julienne strips*

1 onion *sliced*

1 can (10 oz) condensed tomato soup

½ cup sugar

⅓ cup vinegar

salt and pepper *to taste*

1 tbs prepared mustard

Serves 6

METHOD

Place the pepper strips and onion in a bowl with the carrots.

Mix together the soup, sugar, vinegar, salt, pepper and mustard. Pour over the vegetables, stir and refrigerate overnight.

Chicken Salad with Marinated Carrots

PEAS AND RICE

Combining peas and rice in one dish is very common in most Caribbean islands. The most popular peas are yellow split, red kidney, blackeye, lentils or pigeon.

INGREDIENTS

3 cups long grain rice *washed and soaked in water for 2 hours*

½ cup pigeon peas *washed and soaked in water overnight, or* 1 can (16oz) canned variety

½ tsp basil

½ tsp oregano

seasoned salt *to taste*

2 oz salt pork *cut into ½ inch cubes*

4 tbs margarine

Serves 6

METHOD

Drain the peas, place in a saucepan with the seasoned salt, oregano, basil and salt pork and boil until tender but firm.

Drain the rice and add to the pan with enough water to just cover the rice. Stir in the margarine and mix well. Bring to the boil, then reduce the heat to the lowest level, cover and steam until all the water has evaporated. This should take approximately 20–30 minutes.

Serve hot with your favourite meat, poultry or fish dish.

(See **Note** on page 33 re cooking peas/beans.)

BAHAMIAN PEAS AND RICE

This Caribbean staple is prepared a little differently in the Bahamas and because of this I have decided to include it as a separate recipe.

INGREDIENTS

8 oz bacon *cut in strips*

3 tbs butter

1 large onion *chopped*

2 stalks celery *chopped*

2 tomatoes *chopped*

1 orange *or* green bell pepper *chopped*

3 cups long grain rice *soaked in water for at least 2 hours*

1 cup frozen blackeye peas

1 tbs tomato paste

seasoned salt *to taste*

¼ tsp thyme

¼ tsp basil

Serves 6

METHOD

Heat the butter in a saucepan and sauté the onion for about 3 minutes or until it becomes transparent. Add the bacon and continue to stir-fry for another 2 minutes. Stir in the tomatoes, celery and bell pepper and cook for a further two minutes.

Wash and drain the rice, then add it to the saucepan together with the peas, herbs, tomato paste and seasoned salt. Pour in enough water to barely cover the rice, stir well and close the pan. Allow it to come to the boil, then immediately reduce the heat to the lowest level. Let it cook for approximately 30 minutes or until all of the liquid has evaporated. Stir once or twice during the cooking process to prevent sticking and burning.

PHULOURI – SPLIT PEA FRITTERS

These fritters are a welcome snack for both children and adults. They are made with yellow split peas flour and are similar to 'Falafel' from the Middle East. As a matter of fact, I serve them at the trade shows we attend and they have always been a hit! They are so popular that people always ask me to fax them the recipe after returning home.

INGREDIENTS

14 oz split peas flour

1 lb all-purpose flour

2 tsp curry powder

2 tsp roasted ground cumin

3 tsp baking powder

2 tbs granulated garlic

1 tsp salt *or to your taste*

1 tbs hot pepper sauce

4 cups water

vegetable oil *for frying*

Serves 12

METHOD

In a mixing bowl blend all of the dry ingredients together, then mix in the pepper sauce. Add water a little at a time to make a batter of dropping consistency.

Heat some vegetable oil in a wok or deep pan.

With a teaspoon, drop the batter into the wok and fry until golden – approximately 3 minutes.

Serve warm at parties as an hors d'oeuvres or just to accompany drinks.

Note:

Tamarind Sauce is a great dip to accompany these fritters (see recipe, page 47).

PICKLED CUCUMBERS

The flavour of the cucumbers gets better the longer they are allowed to steep in the marinade. You may adjust the heat level to suit your taste.

INGREDIENTS

2 cucumbers

½ tsp salt

½ tsp hot pepper sauce

¼ cup water

1 tbs lime juice

1 tbs vinegar

Serves 6

METHOD

Peel and slice the cucumbers and place in a bowl.

Mix all of the other ingredients together, then pour over the cucumbers and toss. Cover and place in the refrigerator for at least 1 hour before serving.

Note:

The addition of a ripe avocado that has been diced in 1 inch cubes brings new meaning to the word 'wonderful'!

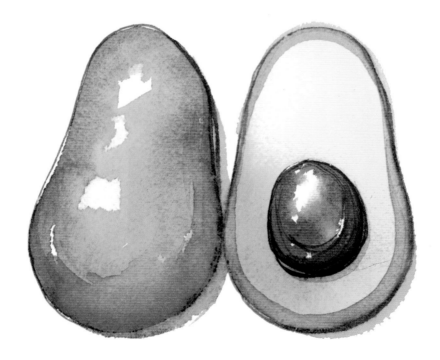

PIG IN A BLANKET

Because Caribbean people are always looking for an excuse to get together with friends, snacks like this one are very popular. These bite-sized delicacies go nicely with some chat and a rum punch.

INGREDIENTS

1 can cocktail sausages

5 ripe plantains

oil *for frying*

Serves 8

METHOD

Peel the plantains and slice them from top to bottom about ⅛ inch thick. Fry until golden in a pan and then drain on paper towel. Cut them in half; roll each sausage in a slice of the fried plantain and secure with a toothpick.

Warm in the microwave just before serving.

PLANTAINS IN CHEESE SAUCE

This dish must be tasted to be truly appreciated. Just reading the recipe does not do it justice. Like breadfruit, plantains are grown in all the islands.

This dish is prepared for special occasions but ripe plantains are fried as a side dish on a regular basis in places like Guyana, Barbados, Belize, Antigua, Dominica, St Lucia, the Virgin Islands and the Cayman Islands. On reflection, there does not appear to be any island that doesn't do it!

INGREDIENTS

vegetable oil *for frying*

3 lb ripe plantains *peeled and sliced lengthwise*

Sauce

3 tbs butter

¼ cup flour

2½ cups milk

1 tsp salt

black pepper *to taste*

2½ cups grated cheddar cheese

Serves 6

METHOD

Heat the oil in a frying pan and add the plantains, frying a few at a time until golden. Drain on paper towel.

Make the sauce by melting the butter in a pan, then sprinkling over the flour. Stir once, then slowly add the milk. Stirring all the time, season to taste with salt and pepper.

Stir in 2 cups of the cheese and allow the sauce to simmer for 3 minutes to thicken.

In a greased oven-proof dish, place a layer of the plantains followed by a layer of the sauce. Repeat, ending with a layer of sauce. Sprinkle over the remaining cheese and bake in a preheated oven, 300 °F, for 1 hour. Much of the sauce should be absorbed by this time.

Serve hot.

POTATO BALLS

These are made in a similar way to Breadfruit Balls but the taste is different.

When my husband visits Guyana he can be found outside the cinemas at half-time patronising the vendors who sell these treats. They ride around on bicycles that have been modified to accommodate a display case and sell a variety of 'goodies' that never ceases to amaze me!

INGREDIENTS

3 lbs potatoes

6 cloves garlic *minced*

1 green onion *minced*

1 onion *minced*

3 eggs *beaten*

1½ cups flour

½ tsp roasted cumin

1 tsp hot pepper sauce

½ tsp salt

breadcrumbs *for rolling*

vegetable oil *for frying*

Serves 10

METHOD

Peel and boil the potatoes in salted water until tender. Mash with a fork (or pass through a potato ricer) and mix in the garlic, onion, salt, pepper sauce, cumin, flour and green onion. Blend in 1 egg. The mixture should be fairly stiff. If it is not, add a little more flour.

Form into balls about 1½ inches in diameter, roll in breadcrumbs, then the remaining beaten egg, and deep fry until golden.

Note:

Here is a variation of this basic recipe:

Hard boil 8 eggs and cut them in half. Flatten the mixture in the palm of your hand and place half an egg in the centre. Bring the edges up to enclose the egg and shape into an oval. Roll in breadcrumbs, then in beaten egg, and deep fry until golden.

PUMPKIN FRITTERS

*The variety of pumpkin served in the Caribbean is the 'Calabaza'.
The skin is green and yellow with the flesh varying from pale
yellow to bright orange.*

These fritters are sometimes even served as a dessert.

INGREDIENTS

1½ lbs pumpkin

1 egg *beaten*

1 tsp baking powder

2 tbsp sugar

¼ tsp ground cinnamon

2 tbsp margarine *melted*

½ cup milk

6 oz flour

vegetable oil *for frying*

sugar *for dusting*

Serves 8

METHOD

Peel and boil the pumpkin, then pass it through a potato ricer.
Add the beaten egg, milk, margarine, sugar, cinnamon, and mix
well.

Fold in the flour and baking powder and beat into a thick
batter.

Heat the oil in a frying pan and drop the batter by the
tablespoonful into the hot oil. Fry until golden brown. Drain on
paper towel, then sprinkle with sugar.

RICE FRITTERS

A quick and easy snack that is very filling. Rice Fritters can be served at any time of the day.

INGREDIENTS

1 cup boiled long grain rice

4 eggs *beaten*

¼ lb raisins

¼ tsp grated lemon peel

1 cup flour

grated nutmeg and sugar *to taste*

vegetable oil *for frying*

Serves 4

METHOD

Mix all of the ingredients together and drop into hot fat. Cook on both sides until golden.

ST VINCENT

St Vincent is the largest of the more than thirty islands that make up St Vincent and the Grenadines.

At the time when the Europeans were busy colonising the other Caribbean islands, they quite sensibly left St Vincent alone. The primary reason for their decision was because of the reputation of the St Vincent Caribs, who never took too kindly to these unwelcome visitors. Furthermore, every time the Caribs from the neighbouring islands lost the battles with the various colonial armies, the survivors fled to St Vincent, swelling their ranks even more.

These Caribs were joined by escaped slaves from Barbados and the inevitable result of their association produced the 'Black Caribs', so named to distinguish them from the original 'Yellow Caribs' who by this time began to worry about losing their dominance and in 1719 made the unprecedented decision of allowing the French to settle on the island. Several exchanges of ownership took place between the British and the French and this continued until 1783 when the Treaty of Versailles gave the English possession of the island.

The French didn't give up so easily and in 1795 supported the Black Caribs, who attacked the British in what became known as the Second Carib War. This war lasted for two years with the British only gaining the upper hand with the death of one of the prominent Carib chiefs in 1796. The Black Caribs eventually gave up their valiant fight in 1797 with the survivors being sent to Belize. As for the Yellow Caribs, they withdrew to the northern part of St Vincent. To their credit, the descendants of both of these groups survive to this day.

Interesting facts about St Vincent and the Grenadines

- The Botanical Gardens were established in 1763 as a commercial breeding ground for exotic plants from all over the world.
- Were it not for the mutiny on board the *HMS Bounty* under the captaincy of William Bligh, the breadfruit plants that were being brought from Tahiti would have arrived there in 1789.
- The plants, one of which eventually arrived in 1793, still lives on through one of its offspring that survives in the garden to this day.

ROAST BREADFRUIT

Common to many of the islands, this version is my favourite. It is usually done while sitting around a camp fire and having a drink!

In St Vincent it is one of their staples and the street vendors roast them 'live'. They are usually picked one day before roasting and turned upside down to drain overnight. The vendors then toss them whole into the bonfire. Many people buy them this way, then take them home to be used in various recipes.

INGREDIENTS

1 large breadfruit *top cut off and centre hollowed out. The hole should be about 3 inches in diameter*

1 small can corned beef

1 small onion *chopped*

2 cloves garlic *minced*

butter

Serves 4

METHOD

Line the hollow with butter. Mix the corned beef, onion and garlic together and stuff it into the hole. Cover in aluminium foil and toss into a camp fire. Roast until a skewer goes through the breadfruit easily.

Note:

It can also be roasted in an oven but the open flame seems to add a little extra 'something' that the oven baked ones lack.

SALTFISH CAKES

This next recipe is one of our most popular hors d'oeuvres. It is made from salted cod and is always included in any Caribbean party where rum is going to be served. In the islands, we like our hors d'oeuvres to be filling – more like mini meals than your usual party favourites . . . you will find things like fish cakes, stuffed eggs, pig in a blanket (which is made from cocktail sausages wrapped in fried plantain), potato balls, egg balls, and the like. By the time you are ready for the main meal, you are sometimes already full from the goodies.

In a few of the islands – the ones that come to mind immediately are Cayman and Jamaica – these are also called 'Stamp N Go'.

INGREDIENTS

4 oz boneless salted cod

3 tbs Barbadian Seasoning (see recipe, page 123)

4 cloves garlic *minced*

1 onion *chopped*

salt *to taste*

1 tbs baking powder

1 lb all-purpose flour

oil *for frying*

1 medium potato *boiled and mashed*

hot pepper sauce to *taste*

Serves 10

METHOD

Boil the salted cod in water for 5 minutes, then drain and cool under running water. Doing this tenderises the fish and reduces the salt content. Shred the fish with your fingers.

Mix together the fish, potato, Barbadian Seasoning, onion, garlic, pepper sauce, baking powder and flour.

Add water to the mix a little at a time until you get the consistency of a thick batter. This is important, because you want your mixture to stay together when you add it to the hot oil.

Adjust the seasonings to taste, and remember you started with salted cod, so you may not have to add much salt, if any at all.

Heat the oil in a wok or deep pan and drop the batter by the teaspoonful into the hot oil.

Fry until golden brown, then drain the excess oil on paper towel and serve warm with Tamarind Sauce (see page 47), fruit chutney or tomato ketchup mixed with hot pepper sauce.

SALTFISH PATTIES

Saltfish Patties, garnished with tomatoes, yellow pepper and green peas

These patties are extremely filling depending on the size – one of these together with a glass of tropical fruit juice or a beer makes a great snack or lunch on any day. My friend Andrea Duguid lived on the Virgin Island of St Thomas for a while and she swears by these patties. She often tells me about the times she would sit outside her favourite haunt to wait until they were finished frying!

INGREDIENTS

8 oz boneless saltfish

1 large onion *chopped*

6 cloves garlic *minced*

1 tbs chopped parsley

½ red bell pepper *chopped*

2 green onions *chopped*

¼ cup water

2 large tomatoes *chopped*

1 tbsp vinegar

½ tsp hot pepper sauce

¼ tsp powdered mustard

3 tbs vegetable oil

1 tbs all-purpose flour

The Crust

4 cups all-purpose flour

1 lb shortening

1 cup cold water

½ tsp salt

1 tsp baking powder

vegetable oil *for frying*

Serves 6

METHOD

Boil the saltfish in water for 5 minutes, then drain and cool under running water. Flake the fish and set aside.

In a pan heat the oil and sauté the onion, garlic and green onions for 2 minutes, or until the onions are transparent. Add the parsley, tomatoes and bell pepper and cook for another 3 minutes. Stir in the fish, mustard, pepper sauce and vinegar and simmer for 2 minutes.

Make a paste with the flour and water and add that to the mixture. Adjust seasonings to your taste. Cook for a further 3 minutes, then remove from the heat and allow to cool before filling the crust.

The Crust

Sift the flour, salt and baking powder together, then cut in the shortening. Add the water, using a fork to blend it in. Shape the dough into a ball and refrigerate for at least 1 hour.

Using a floured rolling pin and board, roll the dough to between ⅛ and ¼ inch thick then cut out 6 inch circles. Fill the centre of each with 2 tablespoons of the fish mixture and fold over. Moisten the bottom lid with water and seal using a fork to press the dough together.

Deep fry in vegetable oil, turning once.

SCALLOPED BREADFRUIT

This is our Caribbean version of scalloped potatoes.

INGREDIENTS

1 breadfruit *peeled, sliced and boiled in salted water*

8 oz cheddar cheese *grated*

2 cups milk

¼ cup flour

¼ cup margarine

seasoned salt *to taste*

1 medium grated onion

½ cup tomato ketchup

1 tbs breadcrumbs

¼ tsp paprika

Serves 6

METHOD

Grease a rectangle oven-proof dish.

Slice the breadfruit into ¼ inch thick slices and set aside.

Melt the margarine in a saucepan then stir in the flour. Pour in the milk and whisk to break up any lumps.

Stir in the cheese, seasoned salt, onion and tomato ketchup. Make sure there are no lumps by stirring briskly with a whisk. Allow the sauce to boil for about 2 minutes, then remove from the heat.

Place a layer of breadfruit in the dish then pour on some sauce. Repeat, ending with sauce. Sprinkle on the breadcrumbs and paprika.

Brown in a preheated oven, 350 °F, for 30 minutes.

Scalloped Breadfruit, garnished with radish and parsley

SAVORY STUFFED PUMPKIN

Excellent at a dinner party or family gathering.

INGREDIENTS

1 pumpkin (about 3–4 lb) *washed and dried*

Stuffing

¼ cup butter

2 large onions *minced*

6 green onions *chopped*

6 cloves garlic *minced*

3 rashers bacon *chopped*

1 tsp hot pepper sauce

1 cups cashew nuts *toasted*

2½ cups breadcrumbs

1 egg *beaten*

seasoned salt *to taste*

2 cups cheddar cheese *grated*

Serves 8

METHOD

First, cut off 2 inches from the top of the pumpkin in a zigzag pattern and reserve for the lid. Scoop out the seeds and discard.

Next, make the stuffing. Heat 2 tablespoons of the butter in a large saucepan and sauté the onion, garlic and green onions for 3 minutes. Add the bacon and continue to cook for another 3 minutes. Stir in the cashews, breadcrumbs, pepper sauce, egg, seasoned salt and cheese.

Remove from the heat.

Fill the pumpkin shell with the stuffing. Dot with butter and replace the lid.

Place on a baking sheet and cook in a preheated oven at 350 °F for 1½ hours, or until the pumpkin is cooked.

Savoury Stuffed Pumpkin

ST LUCIA

St Lucia's official language is English, although you may find this very hard to believe if you ever happen to overhear two St Lucians in an animated conversation, or meet two of the older vendors in the market. For St Lucian history is based on an endless fight between the British and the French for possession of the island. From the time that St Lucia was first (formally) settled in 1605 until it was ceded to the British in 1814, the island changed hands no less than fourteen times. It isn't difficult to figure out why the 'real' language of St Lucia is a combination of English and French.

Interesting fact about St Lucia
- St Lucia is the birthplace of Derek Walcott, the 1992 Nobel Prize Winner for Literature.

ST LUCIAN STEW PEAS

It is truly amazing how the cuisine of the Caribbean islands evolved. This recipe is the version of stewed kidney beans ('peas') that is commonly cooked in St Lucia. Although there is a similarity between this and the Jamaican version, the difference is enough to justify its inclusion as part of this collection.

INGREDIENTS

2 cups red kidney beans *soaked overnight*

salt *to taste*

1 tsp hot pepper sauce

1 large onion *chopped*

5 cloves garlic *minced*

¼ tsp marjoram

¼ tsp thyme

¼ tsp basil

2 stalks celery *chopped*

1 oz fresh cilantro (coriander) *chopped*

2 tbs margarine

4 cups water

Serves 6

METHOD

Place all of the ingredients (except the margarine) in a saucepan and bring to the boil. Reduce the heat and simmer until the peas are tender.

Stir in the margarine and continue to cook for a further 5 minutes.

(See **Note** on page 33 re cooked peas/beans)

St Lucian Beef Stew, Foo Foo, St Lucian Stew Peas and boiled rice

SWEET POTATO AND CHANNA NESTS

This recipe comes from Guyana and is a special treat at a dinner party or other formal occasion.

INGREDIENTS

2 lb sweet potatoes

2 oz butter

1 small onion *chopped*

½ cup milk

2 cans (16 oz) channa or chick peas *drained* (Garbanzo)

1 oz butter *to glaze*

1 egg yolk *to glaze*

Serves 6

METHOD

Wash, peel and cook the sweet potatoes in salted water.

Meanwhile heat the milk and keep it hot.

Once cooked, drain the sweet potatoes and put through a potato ricer. Mix with the butter and just enough milk to give a firm piping consistency.

Allow to cool.

For the Nests . . .

Make round bases with about 1 tablespoon of the sweet potato mixture on a greased baking sheet then, using a ⅜ inch meringue Star Tube in a forcing bag, pipe the mixture around the edge of the base to form a nest about 1½ inch deep.

Place in a preheated oven at 350 °F for 5 minutes to slightly harden the edges. Then remove from the oven and brush with egg yolk.

When ready to serve, fill with channa which has been tossed in butter and chopped onion. Return to the oven for 3 minutes before serving.

Sweet Potato and Channa Nests

SWEET POTATO PIE

The sweet potato is found in every island of the Caribbean and, just like the breadfruit, it is used in many ways. This pie can be found on the table at Christmas-time and when families gather to share a meal on special occasions.

INGREDIENTS

4 lb sweet potatoes

2 cups crushed pineapple

1 tsp seasoned salt

4 pineapple rings

4 maraschino cherries

margarine (optional)

Serves 8

METHOD

Peel and boil the sweet potatoes in salted water until tender. Mash them, then mix in the crushed pineapple and salt. Add a little margarine if the mixture is too stiff.

Grease an oven-proof dish and place the mixture in it. Decorate the top with pineapple rings and a maraschino cherry in the centre of each.

Bake in a preheated oven at 350 °F for 30 minutes.

TROPICAL COLESLAW

Try this slaw with any kind of Bar-B-Q.

INGREDIENTS

2 cups shredded cabbage

1 cup shredded carrots

1 cup pineapple chunks

½ cup raisins

¼ cup mayonnaise

¼ cup evaporated milk

1 tbs sugar

½ tsp salt

Serves 8

METHOD

Toss the cabbage, carrots, pineapple and raisins together in a salad bowl. Make the dressing by mixing the mayonnaise, milk, sugar and salt. Pour into the salad bowl and mix well.

Chill in the refrigerator for at least 1 hour before serving.

Okras Cook-up Rice and Tropical Coleslaw, garnished with four pieces of pig's tail

YAM PIE

As mentioned before, ground provisions (root crops) are consumed in large quantities by the people of the Caribbean. The way to keep the cooking interesting is to invent new ways to serve an old staple – hope you like this recipe as much as my family does.

INGREDIENTS

4 lb yams *boiled and mashed*

3 tbs vegetable oil

2 medium onions *chopped*

5 rashers bacon

½ cup milk

1 tsp seasoned salt

¼ cup margarine

1 tsp hot pepper sauce

½ cup grated cheddar cheese

½ tsp paprika

Serves 8

METHOD

Heat the oil in a pan and sauté the onions for 2 minutes. Add the bacon and continue to stir-fry for a further 3 minutes.

In a large bowl, mix the mashed yam with the margarine, milk, seasoned salt and pepper sauce, then stir in the bacon and onions.

Grease an oven-proof dish then pour in the yam mixture. Level with a spoon and sprinkle the grated cheese and paprika on top.

Bake in a preheated oven, 350 °F, for 30 minutes, or until golden brown.

Yam Pie, garnished with sticks of red pepper

desserts and baked goods

BAKES (JOHNNY CAKES)

In places like the Bahamas and the Virgin Islands this is a staple. Originally they were called 'Journey Cakes' because in the old days they were ideal for taking on long trips. In many islands the addition of ½ cup raisins and ¼ cup sugar changes them into a fritter that children adore.

In my household it is not unusual for my two children to devour about 20 between them.

INGREDIENTS

1 lb all purpose-flour

1 tsp baking powder

½ tsp salt

2 tbs margarine

2 tbs sugar

water *to mix*

vegetable oil *for frying*

Serves 4

METHOD

Sift the flour, baking powder and salt together. Rub in the fat, then add the sugar. Pour in a little water and mix to a stiff consistency. Knead on a floured board for 5 minutes.

Shape the mixture into circles about 2 inches in diameter and ½ inch thick. Deep fry in hot oil on both sides until golden.

Drain on paper towel before serving with meat or fish, cheese or jam.

BANANA BREAD

A special treat at any time of the day.
  Many families have a banana tree out back and when the fruit is ripe what a great way to use some up!

INGREDIENTS

4 oz butter

1 cup sugar

2 cups flour

3 tsp baking powder

3 ripe bananas *crushed*

2 eggs

Each loaf will serve 8

METHOD

Cream the butter and sugar for 15 minutes. Add the eggs, then the crushed bananas. Mix the baking powder and the flour, then add to the mixture.

  Grease two loaf tins and divide the mixture between them. Bake in a preheated oven at 300 °F for approximately 1 hour.

Banana Bread with slices of banana, grape and cherry

BANANA FLAMBÉ

In places like the Bahamas, Jamaica, Barbados and the Virgin Islands this dessert is very well known. It is usually done in restaurants 'live' at the dinner table and is quite an impressive sight.

INGREDIENTS

2 ripe bananas *peeled and sliced lengthways down the middle*

¼ cup icing sugar

2 tbs butter

¼ cup pineapple juice mixed with 1 tsp cornstarch

¼ cup rum

Serves 2

METHOD

Heat the butter in a frying pan and add the sugar. Stir until it is melted and begins to bubble.

Gently place the bananas in the pan and cook each side for 1 minute. Pour in the juice, mix and heat through until the sauce bubbles and thickens.

Warm the rum in a separate pan and pour over the bananas. Set it alight immediately.

Serve with ice cream, and garnish with fruit of your choice.

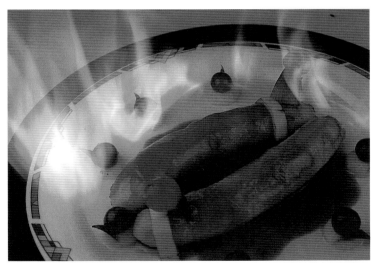

Banana Flambé

BREAD PUDDING

In the Caribbean, nothing gets wasted . . . and this is particularly true when it comes to Bread Pudding. It is traditionally made with bread that has gone stale but in recent times, with the increasing fortunes of many households, fresh bread is used. This is the way it is prepared in the Virgin Islands, Guyana and Barbados.

INGREDIENTS

2 loaves sliced bread

½ cup melted margarine

¼ cup melted shortening

3 eggs *beaten*

12 oz sugar

4 cups milk

2 cup raisins

½ cup rum

½ tsp nutmeg

½ tsp cinnamon

1 tbs vanilla essence

Serves 10

METHOD

Break the bread into pieces and soak in the milk for 10 minutes. Add the beaten eggs, rum, melted shortening and margarine. Mix well.

Next, blend in all of the remaining ingredients and pour into a greased pan.

Brush the top with a glaze of sugar and water (½ cup water mixed with 3 tablespoons sugar) and bake in a preheated oven at 325 °F for 1 hour, or until a skewer comes out clean when inserted.

Serve warm with Rum Sauce, (see page 171).

RUM SAUCE

INGREDIENTS

1 cup brown sugar

4 oz butter

3 egg whites

⅛ tsp salt

¼ cup rum

8 oz whipped cream

METHOD

Place the sugar, butter, salt and egg whites in the top of a double boiler and cook, stirring constantly until the mixture reaches the consistency of salad dressing.

Allow the sauce to cool for at least 1 hour, then stir in the rum and fold in the whipped cream.

CHRISTMAS

If you had to rate the Caribbean's most popular celebration, Christmas would win by a mile, for this is the time of year that everyone (both children and adults) looks forward to. This is the time when all your friends that you haven't seen all year are sure to visit, the time when children in even the lowliest household can expect to receive a treasured gift, even if their birthdays were overlooked earlier in the year.

The season begins around the first of November with a trickle of Christmas music being played on the radio stations, and the first Christmas advertisements beginning to appear on TV. The air begins to chill and it is not unusual for night time temperatures to dip to a low 70 degrees Fahrenheit making everyone complain about the 'cold'.

As the season progresses more and more traditional Christmas music is heard and we start to 'Dream of a White Christmas' as we sing along to the old time favourites like Bing Crosby and Nat King Cole . . . but don't for a moment begin to think that we don't have our very own Christmas repertoire, ranging from soulful ballads like 'Kiss me for Christmas' to jumpy Christmas music like 'Santa got a Sun Burn'.

Soon after, paint sales skyrocket as everyone gives the house a 'brush up' for Christmas. The owners of the fabric stores lick their chops in anticipation of the miles of cloth that will be needed to recover cushions and make new drapes, while the more affluent will certainly invest in a new carpet for their 'front house' (living room). Christmas is the time that we celebrate the birth of Christ so everything must be just right.

Everyone has a reason to go shopping, be it for clothes to wear to the inevitable parties or to church on Christmas morning, or be it to choose toys for little ones.

When it is almost Christmas the 'front house' is open to all ... the special chairs that were out of bounds all year are now available for sitting in. Lots of liquor is consumed as friends and family visit other friends and family (without the help of any MCI program) and the house begins to smell really nice with the imported Christmas trees from North America.

If you haven't 'engaged' your leg of pork by now, you will be in a frantic scramble, for pork is in demand during the season. Engaging pork simply means to request it in advance from a countryside farmer – it has nothing to do with marrying a pig! It isn't unusual for a pig to have ten legs as the farmer with only one pig to his name merrily accepts all bookings for his meat . . .

House parties (private parties) are the norm at this time of year – all week long someone somewhere is holding a party and if you happen to receive more than one invitation for the same night you simply split your time between each one.

As the big day approaches the houses are all alive with Christmas lights and laughter, as friends remember old times and gather round to sing Christmas carols. This is the time that Pepperpot and Garlic Pork are prepared and the extra ham, not the special Christmas Day ham but the one to serve to visitors, makes its appearance.

At some point around this time, you will need to escape all the visiting friends, as you stack the car with presents, and take the kids to deliver, and hopefully receive, their Christmas goodies. This is one of the few occasions that you will make prior visiting arrangements, since everyone is busy visiting everyone else and you want to make sure that your friends are at home when you get there.

Come Christmas Eve, the house will be smelling like heaven as the baking starts in earnest. The list is long and the hard work is sure to be interrupted by visiting friends with nothing better to do but drink your liquor and shoot the breeze, but the spirit of the occasion and the spirits of the liquor keep you going. Sometime between Christmas Eve and early Christmas morning you will be roasting turkey, chicken and pork as well as baking ham, cleaning the house, installing curtains, replacing cushion covers, and drinking. If you are lucky, you'll get a few minutes in between to go and annoy someone else.

The only thing not yet mentioned, and by far the most important, is the Christmas cake – for, long before the Christmas season begins, many households have already mixed their fruit and added a large amount of rum, port wine and falernum, before carefully putting the mixture to soak in a safe place 'til Christmas Eve night.

Once the Christmas cake is baked, and all the washing up completed, it is time to catch a couple of winks before setting off for the traditional 5 am church service.

On returning from church it is time to finish preparation for the big Christmas Day lunch, before your guests arrive – for either your close friends or family are sure to be invited to share in the feast.

By the time that lunch is finished everyone but the children are ready to catch a nap before the next session starts sometime later in the evening.

Caribbean Rum Cake with custard and Sorrel Drink

INGREDIENTS

8 oz raisins

8 oz currants

1 lb pitted prunes

1 lb glace cherries *cut into quarters*

8 oz mixed peel

8 oz pitted dates

1 lb flour

12 oz brown sugar

6 eggs

1 lb margarine

¼ cup gravy browning

4 oz shelled walnuts *broken into quarters*

4 oz flaked almonds

¼ tsp powdered cloves

½ tsp powdered cinnamon

2 tbs vanilla or mixed essence

1½ pints rum

1½ pints cake mix *or* port wine

Each cake will serve 10

CARIBBEAN RUM CAKE

This cake was traditionally baked at Christmas or for special occasions, for example, weddings, christenings or anniversaries. I believe this was because of the cost of putting it together. Even today it is still a treat to be offered a piece of this cake in the middle of the year.

METHOD

Preparation – at least two weeks prior to baking

In a food processor grind half the raisins, half the currants, prunes, mixed peel and dates. Place **all** the fruit in a large glass jar. Pour over the rum, and 1 pint of the wine. Mix well, cover and leave to stand for at least two weeks before baking.

To bake...

Cream the margarine and sugar for 20 minutes, until light and the sugar is almost dissolved. Add the eggs one at a time and mix well with each addition. Pour in the ground fruit, fruit, cherries, nuts, cloves, cinnamon, essence and gravy browning. Stir many times to make sure that the fruit is evenly distributed. Add the flour a little at a time making sure to break up any lumps. (See **Note** below).

Grease and flour two medium springform pans and divide the mixture between the two. Bake in a preheated 325 °F oven for 1 hour, or until an inserted skewer comes out clean. With a skewer, immediately stick holes all over the cake and pour on the remaining wine.

Allow to cool completely, then wrap in plastic film and foil for storage. This cake can remain in storage for over a year.

Decorate with marzipan and royal icing, if desired. It has been my experience that lots of people like it plain.

Note:

The secret to success in making this cake is knowing exactly how much flour to add. Stir in the flour a little at a time and do the following test to see when you have the correct consistency.

Stand a wooden spoon in the centre of the mixture. It should stand upright then slowly start to fall. If it falls too quickly you should add an ounce or two at a time and repeat the test.

CASSAVA PONE

In days of old when the main food source for the slaves was root crops, they invented some ingenious ways to use what was available. In many of the islands this next recipe is known as 'Cassava Pone' but in the Cayman Islands it is referred to as 'Cayman Heavy Cake'.

INGREDIENTS

4 lb grated cassava (yucca)

1 lb sugar

1 tsp allspice

1 tsp cinnamon

1 tsp nutmeg

1 tsp grated orange peel

2 tsp salt

1 coconut *grated,* or 12 oz
dessicated coconut

½ lb raisins

½ lb butter

¼ lb shortening

2 tsp vanilla essence

2 eggs

1 cup evaporated milk

1 cup water

Glaze
½ cup sugar
½ cup water

Serves 12

METHOD

Make a glaze by dissolving ½ cup sugar and ½ cup water.

Mix all of the dry ingredients together. Beat the eggs and add to the milk. Melt the butter and shortening, then add the essence. Mix everything together and pour into greased pan. Glaze with the sugar and water mixture and bake immediately in a preheated oven at 325 °F for 1½ hours.

Note:

If cassava is not available you may use any other starchy vegetable, like potatoes, yams and so on . . .

CHOCOLATE CAKE

It was the Maya Indians in Belize who first discovered how to process the beans from the cacao tree into what they called the 'Food Of The Gods'. This substance was considered to be so precious that by law only the nobility were allowed to eat it.

Thanks to that ancient civilisation, we can now make this gooey, fudgey, super-moist chocolate cake that the entire family will enjoy!

INGREDIENTS

2 cups all-purpose flour

2 cups sugar

1 cup mayonnaise

3 eggs

1 cup cocoa

2 cups black coffee *cooled*

2 tsp baking powder

Topping

1 can condensed milk

¾ cup sifted cocoa

Serves 10

METHOD

Place all of the ingredients together in a large bowl and beat with a mixer until smooth and the sugar has dissolved.

Bake in a greased pan for approximately 1 hour in a pre-heated 350 °F oven.

Topping

Mix the cocoa and milk together in a double boiler. Stir frequently over medium heat. The topping is finished when it becomes very thick and fudgey. This should take between 20 and 30 minutes.

Then pour the topping over the top and sides of the cake and spread with the blade of a knife or spatula.

COCONUT BREAD

This recipe was given to me by my Barbadian friend, Mary Johnson. It is the best I have ever tasted and, even if you have never attempted baking before, this one is so easy and tastes so good you'll do it every week. Trust me . . .

INGREDIENTS

4 lb self-raising flour

26 oz granulated sugar

1½ lb grated coconut, *or* 1 lb dessicated

1 lb melted margarine

4 large eggs

3 tbs mixed essence *or* 1½ tsp each vanilla and almond essence

4 oz raisins

8 oz glacé cherries

3 oz sliced almonds (optional)

Each loaf will serve 8

METHOD

In a bowl, mix together the flour, 24 oz sugar, 1 lb of coconut, the raisins, cherries and almonds. Pour in the melted margarine and continue to mix. I find it easier to do this with my hands.

Beat the eggs lightly and add 2 tbs essence. Pour into the bowl and blend well. Divide the dough into four equal parts and knead each piece very lightly for 1 minute. Do not overdo this step because it will cause the bread to become too stiff.

Grease and flour four 2 lb loaf tins and shape each piece to fit the tin before placing it in. Now mix together the remaining ½ lb of grated coconut, 2 oz sugar and 1 tablespoon essence. Make a gutter-like opening about 1½ inches wide and 1 inch deep in the dough for the entire length of the pan.

Divide this mixture into four equal parts and sprinkle it into each gutter. Pull the dough together to close it. Pat it to make sure the coconut is sealed inside the pocket.

With a knife, make three diagonal cuts in the top of each loaf and bake in a preheated 300 °F oven for 1 hour, or until an inserted skewer comes out clean. (Another way to check whether it is ready is to press the loaf lightly with your finger tips: when done it will spring back into its original shape.)

Coconut Bread

CONKIES AND GUY FAWKES

Just as many Caribbean festivals are a combination of African and European cultures, the same blend frequently applies to our food. Much of this was developed by adapting African and European recipes using locally-available ingredients and lots of imagination. In the case of Conkies and Guy Fawkes Day, this adaptation crossed both the cultural and culinary boundaries in Barbados.

Back in 1605, a group of Catholic Englishmen decided to change the religious direction of England by blowing up the House of Commons while the King and his chief ministers were present. To accomplish this, they recruited Guy Fawkes, another Englishman who had been fighting with the Spaniards and who had the necessary military experience, to help the plot succeed. At first they tried to dig a tunnel from an adjacent building but, since this was easier said than done, they settled for renting a building which had a cellar that went under the House of Commons. Guy Fawkes had already positioned the required amount of gunpowder (at least 20 barrels which he covered in coals) when the plot was discovered and he was arrested on the evening of 4 November 1605, just one day before the plot was to be carried out. In those days there were several ways of persuading people to talk and Guy Fawkes eventually named all his fellow conspirators. He was executed on 31 January 1606 just opposite the Parliament buildings.

5 November became known as Guy Fawkes Day and was 'celebrated' throughout Britain and, later, many of the colonies, with fireworks and bonfires.

Several years after Guy Fawkes' failed attempt, Britain had colonised a few of the Caribbean islands and the slave trade had begun in earnest. Many of the slaves were brought to the Caribbean from Ghana, where there were two yam festivals each year, one in June and the other in November.

One of the highlights of the yam festival was the making and sharing of Kenke, a dessert made from yams (of course), corn and flour which was wrapped in banana leaves and steamed. Over the course of the years in Barbados the yam festival and Guy Fawkes Day both continued to be celebrated in November and the Kenke, now referred to as Conkie, became synonymous with Guy Fawkes Day. Thus two diverse customs became one, a situation which persisted until Barbados became independent on 30 November 1966 and Guy Fawkes Day ceased to be celebrated. The custom of making and sharing conkies in November nevertheless continues to this day – it is now done as part of the Independence Day celebrations!

CONKIES

Conkies, garnished with radish, parsley and carrot slice

This is how Conkies are made in Barbados to this day. The finished product is served either warm or cold, wrapped in banana leaves. It is similar in appearance to the Pastelle from Trinidad which has its origins in Spain. However, unlike the Pastelle, the Conkie contains no meat.

Duckanoo or Blue Drawers is the name given to this delicacy by Jamaicans. The reason for this is the blue colour that is transferred to the pudding from the banana leaf.

In the Virgin Islands they are known as Chigger Foot Mary. Chiggers are small mites that burrow under the skin and labourers who toil in the fields are their main target.

INGREDIENTS

12 oz pumpkin *peeled and grated*

8 oz sweet potato *peeled and grated*

12 oz brown sugar

1 lb fresh grated coconut *or* 12 oz
    desiccated

1 tsp cinnamon

½ tsp nutmeg

2 tbs almond essence

6 oz raisins

1 cup all-purpose flour

2 cups cornmeal

4 oz margarine *melted*

1 tsp salt

2 oz shortening *melted*

1 cup milk

about 15 eight x ten-inch rectangles
    of young plantain *or* banana
    leaves.

vegetable oil

Serves 10

METHOD

Pass the leaves over an open flame on both sides then wipe them with a damp cloth. The leaves can also be soaked in boiling water for 1 minute. Doing this makes them flexible so that they can be folded easily without tearing. Rub each piece with a little vegetable oil.

Mix the coconut, pumpkin, sweet potato, raisins, sugar and spices together. Add the essence, flour, cornmeal and salt and blend well. Stir in the melted fat and milk and mix until smooth.

Place 2 tablespoons of the mixture in the centre of each square and fold to make a packet. Tie with cord.

Steam on a rack over boiling water for 1 hour, or until firm.

Note:

Corn shucks can be substituted for the banana leaves.

PASTELLES

This is the Pastelle from Trinidad that I told you about earlier (see page 179) which, although similar to the Conkie, has a Spanish origin and is filled with meat. It is similar to the Mexican Tamale.

INGREDIENTS

4 banana leaves

Dough

3 cups cornmeal

3 tbs lard *or* shortening – *cut up*

½ cup oil

2 tsp salt

Filling

2 tbs oil

1 large onion *minced*

4 cloves garlic *minced*

1 tsp hot pepper sauce

½ lb stewing pork *ground*

½ lb stewing beef *ground*

1 tsp thyme

1 tsp basil

1 green onion *minced*

2 tomatoes *peeled and chopped*

4 tbs Worcestershire sauce

seasoned salt *to taste*

¾ cup water

Serves 12

METHOD

Sauté the onion and garlic in the oil for a few minutes, then add the beef, pork, Worcestershire sauce, pepper sauce, green onion, thyme, basil, and seasoned salt. Cook for about 15 minutes, stirring constantly.

Stir in the tomatoes, add the water and bring to the boil. Reduce heat and simmer for 30 minutes, or until all the liquid has evaporated. Adjust seasonings to taste.

To make the dough, place the cornmeal in a large mixing bowl and add the shortening, oil and salt. Pour in 2¾ cups hot water and mix to a smooth dough. Divide the dough into 18 balls.

Pass the banana leaves over an open flame or place them in a bowl and pour boiling water over them.

To make the pastelles so that they fold easily without breaking, dry the leaves then cut into 8 x 10 inch rectangles.

Rub a leaf-rectangle with a little vegetable oil. Flatten one of the dough balls in the palm of your hand to form a circle 4 inches in diameter. Press the outside edges to make then slightly thinner than the rest of the round. Place two tablespoons of the filling in the centre and pull the outer edges of the dough together to seal. Place seam down on the greased banana leaf, then fold the leaf over to form a package. Tie with string. Repeat the process.

Put the meat-filled packages on a rack in a saucepan with water and steam for 1½ hours. Remove the string and leaf before serving hot or cold.

Note:

Corn shucks can be substituted for the banana leaves.

GUAVA DUFF

A favourite in the Bahamas and Jamaica, I hope you will enjoy it also!

INGREDIENTS

2 oz butter

1 cup sugar

3 eggs *beaten*

2 cups guava pulp

½ tsp ground nutmeg

½ tsp ground cinnamon

¼ tsp ground cloves

3 cups flour

2 tsp baking powder

Serves 8

METHOD

Cream together the butter and sugar for about 20 minutes, then add the eggs and continue to mix for a further 5 minutes. Blend in the guava pulp, nutmeg, cinnamon and cloves.

Sift together the flour and baking powder, then fold it into the mixture. Pour the mixture into the top of a greased double boiler and steam for approximately 2 hours, or until an inserted skewer comes out clean.

Serve warm with Rum Sauce (see page 171).

SPICY CHEESE STRAWS

The cheddar cheese used in this recipe comes from England and the flavour is very different from the American variety. These tasty snacks are made by passing a savoury cheese mixture through a cookie press or a large cake decorating tube. The secret to getting this one right is in the mixing of the ingredients. Follow the instructions to the letter then refrigerate the mixture not in the cookie press. I have found that any kind of heat prevents it from coming through the press and then . . . all is lost.

INGREDIENTS

½ lb cheddar cheese *grated*

½ lb softened margarine

1 lb flour

1 tsp baking powder

1 tsp prepared mustard

1 tsp salt

1 tsp hot pepper sauce

Serves 8

METHOD

Mix the margarine, cheese and mustard together. Add the flour, salt, pepper sauce and baking powder.

Pass through a cookie press on to un-greased cookie sheet. (Refrigerate any mixture that is not actually in the cookie press until you are ready for it.)

Bake in a preheated oven at 350 °F for about 10 minutes, or until lightly browned.

Spicy Cheese Straws

JAMAICA

Having accidentally discovered Jamaica in 1494 Columbus and his followers did their usual. They checked to see if the island possessed any large deposits of gold or other precious metals and then, finding none, hastily departed leaving only a small settlement near St Ann's Bay . . . so, when the English attacked Jamaica in 1655, the Spanish gave it up without a fight.

In doing so, the Spanish failed to realise the strategic importance of the island. Hence, Port Royal, not without some encouragement from the government of King Charles of England, quickly developed into a buccaneer stronghold where, from its protected harbour, they could launch their attacks on the Spanish treasure ships.

With all that easy money in circulation, Port Royal soon became one the richest cities in the Americas. Hard working types like those who frequented the city needed entertainment and the resulting abundance of prostitutes and rum shops soon gave Port Royal the reputation as the most sinful city on earth. Many must have viewed it as retribution from above when most of the city sank during an earthquake in 1692. A new city – Kingston, the capital of Jamaica since 1872 – was built to replace it.

Interesting facts about Jamaica
- Tia Maria and Blue Mountain Coffee originated in Jamaica.
- Jamaica is the birthplace of Reggae music.

JAMAICAN EASTER BUN

At Easter-time the bakeries in Jamaica can't make enough of these. A friend of mine who distributes Caribbean foods in Miami and New York is kept buzzing trying to get enough of these buns into stores before Good Friday.

INGREDIENTS

2½ lb flour

¼ lb raisins

¼ lb currants

¼ lb mixed peel

¼ lb glacé cherries *chopped*

1 packet yeast

1 nutmeg *grated*

1 pt warm milk

½ lb butter

1 cup brown sugar

1 cup water

½ tsp ground cinnamon

½ tsp ground allspice

1 tsp salt

1 egg

Serves 8

METHOD

Dissolve the yeast in a little warm water. Next, bring 1 cup of water to the boil, then add the milk.

Place the sugar, salt, butter, cinnamon and allspice in a bowl, then pour in the hot liquid. Beat the egg and add to this mixture.

Sieve half of the flour into the bowl and mix well. Add the yeast and fruit and continue to mix.

Sieve in enough of the remainder of the flour to make a stiff consistency, cover and leave to rise until doubled in size. This should take about 45 minutes.

Turn on to a floured board and knead for about 2 minutes, then add the remaining flour and continue to knead for a few more minutes.

Shape into buns, place on a greased cookie sheet, cover and let them rise until doubled in size (about 30 minutes) .

Bake in a preheated oven at 350 °F until springy to the touch.

PITCH LAKE CAKE

This cake gets its name form the Pitch Lake in Trinidad, and is an ideal desert to prepare a day or two before it is needed.

INGREDIENTS

1 sponge cake *cut into slices then into 1½ inch squares*

⅔ cup coffee liqueur

¼ cup milk

2 cups whipped cream

Filling

8 oz baking chocolate

1 tbs instant coffee

5 eggs *separated*

pinch of salt

1 tbs water

Serves 8

METHOD

Mix the coffee liqueur with the milk in a bowl.

Line the base of an 8 inch springform cake pan with wax paper then cover with a layer of cake slices. Cut the pieces to fit in patchwork fashion. Sprinkle over ⅓ of the liqueur mixture, then cover with the chocolate filling (see below).

Continue making layers this way, ending with a layer of cake and liqueur. Cover the top with plastic wrap and put into the fridge overnight.

Loosen the sides with a knife then take out of the mould. Place a serving platter on top of cake and invert .

Finally, cover the top and sides with whipped cream and decorate with chocolate or fruit.

Filling

To make the filling place the chocolate, coffee and 1 tbs water in a double boiler and cook for 5 minutes, or until the chocolate is melted. Remove from the heat and let the mixture cool slightly.

Then beat in the egg yolks one at a time.

Add the salt to the egg whites and beat until they form peaks. Fold into the chocolate mixture and set aside.

Pitch Lake Cake, decorated with cherries, whipped cream, apple and orange

PLANTAIN CHIPS

While growing up, receiving a handful of these was equivalent to getting a dozen cookies. It was not unusual to get caught with our hands in the 'Plantain Chip Jar'.

INGREDIENTS
6 green plantains
salt *to taste*
oil *for frying*

METHOD
Peel the plantains and thinly slice them in rounds.

Heat the oil and deep fry the slices until crispy and golden. Drain on paper towel and sprinkle with salt.

Note:
These chips are eaten as a snack and can be kept for long periods in an air-tight jar.

drinks

FIRING A GROG

One of the favourite pastimes in the Caribbean is 'Firing a Grog', which really means to drink a liquor (usually rum). The word 'grog' actually appears in the Oxford Dictionary and is defined as 'to have a drink of spirit (rum) and water.' This all came about because of an admiral of the British Navy in the West Indies who wore a grogram coat – a coat made from a coarse fabric of silk and mohair. It seems that this admiral became concerned about drunkenness and indiscipline in the Royal Navy and, sometime in 1731, ordered all rum rations to be diluted. Because of his favourite coat he was called 'Old Grog' and his diluted drink became known as 'Grog' to all concerned. So, even today, in the Caribbean we continue to Fire a Grog whenever the occasion warrants.

RUM

Barbados was the first producer of rum in the world, with historical records attesting to the production of rumbullion on the island as early as 1703. The rumbullion was made by heating a mixture of fermented sugar-cane molasses in simple pot stills. Although the equipment has changed somewhat in the intervening years, many of the original methods and processes are still in use today.

The molasses is produced during the sugar manufacturing process. This molasses is mixed with water and a special yeast and placed in a huge vat where, in just 24 hours with lots of bubbling and foaming, the yeast converts all the sugar in the molasses to alcohol. At the end of this process what is left in the vat is called simply 'wash'.

I must admit that I can't help thinking of dirty laundry when I think of 'wash'.

It is this 'wash' which is distilled in pot stills. While I won't pretend to know much about distilling, there are apparently two types of still in use, one using the original technology which produces a heavier liquor and the other – newer – known as the coffey still, which produces a lighter liquor with a higher alcoholic content.

The alcohol which is produced as a result is crystal clear. It is then diluted and sold as White Rum. To produce the Golden or Dark Rum, the White Rum is first diluted and then placed in oak barrels which are charred on the inside. There it is aged for a minimum of three years (it improves with time). The wood from which the barrel is made gives the rum its golden colour and its mellow taste.

At the appropriate time the rum is taken from the barrels and blended. The job of the master blender is probably the most important of all – for only he holds the secret of the blend. He is the only person to possess the knowledge of choosing the right spirits to blend together and in what quantities.

BARBADIAN RUM PUNCH

Barbadian Rum Punch

Do not let the pleasant taste fool you . . . it carries the kick of a mule!

This is the traditional recipe for Barbadian Rum Punch which is never made in quantities of less than a gallon and is always served ice cold. The sweetness of the sugar and the sourness of the lime cleverly disguise the punch that it will give you after a few drinks. In case you drink up your supply and in your liquorised state find that you are having difficulty with the formula, this clever little rhyme will put you on the right track. It is one of the country's national treasures in literature and it goes like this:

One of Sour,
Two of Sweet,
Three of Strong
And four of Weak.

. . . *Well if it isn't yet a national treasure, it should be.*

The poem represents the proportions of Sour (lime juice), Sweet (simple syrup), Strong (rum) and Weak (water).

Here goes the translation:

INGREDIENTS

3 oz lime juice
6 oz simple syrup
9 oz rum
12 oz water
grated nutmeg
a few dashes of Angostura Bitters

Serves 4

METHOD

In a jug, blend the ingredients with the exception of the nutmeg. Serve in a glass with lots of ice. Sprinkle the nutmeg on the surface.

BANANA DAIQUIRI

With one of these at your side, there is no better way to just kick back, relax and watch the sun go down.

INGREDIENTS

½ cup rum

2 tbs caster sugar

3 tbs lemon juice

1 large banana *cut into thirds*

2 cups crushed ice

2 dashes Angostura Bitters

2 marachino cherries and 2
   pineapple slices *to decorate*

Serves 2

METHOD

Place all of the ingredients (except the cherries and pineapples) into a blender and process for 30 seconds. Pour into two cocktail glasses and decorate with pineapple slices and cherries. Serve immediately.

Banana Daiquiri

GINGER BEER

Caribbean people are so attached to this drink that many soft drink companies bottle it commercially.

INGREDIENTS
4 oz fresh ginger
12 pints hot water
25 whole cloves
simple syrup

METHOD
Wash and scrape the ginger, then grate it. Place in a jar together with the cloves and pour over the water. Cover and leave for 2 days. Strain and add syrup to taste.

PEANUT PUNCH

This one is addictive . . .
My husband loves peanut butter and this punch just fuels his
passion!

INGREDIENTS

1 oz smooth peanut butter

1 cup milk

1½ oz sugar

Serves 1

METHOD

Blend the milk and peanut butter slowly. Whisk in the sugar and
serve immediately over crushed ice.

POOR MAN LIQUEUR

I really like the name of this drink. We call it poor man liqueur because it is made from the cheapest liquor available in the Caribbean.

INGREDIENTS
rind from 1 green lime
2 tbs sugar
3 oz rum
Serves 2

METHOD
Peel the lime. Bend and twist the peel to release the oil. Place in an oven-proof dish with the sugar. Pour in the rum and light with a match. Stir to dissolve the sugar keeping the peel submerged at all times. Do this for about 3 minutes, then extinguish the flame by covering the dish.

Serve immediately – while it's still warm.

PONCHE de CRÈME

Christmas in Trinidad and Barbados would not be the same without the island version of egg-nog. A few days before Christmas it is made and refrigerated . . . the challenge here is to resist consuming all before the big day arrives!

INGREDIENTS

4 cups milk

1 lime

6 eggs *beaten*

1 cup sugar

3 cups rum

1 tbs mixed essence

1 tsp Angostura Bitters

grated nutmeg

METHOD

Peel the lime and place it in a saucepan with the milk. Warm the milk for about 5 minutes, then add the eggs and sugar. Cook the mixture over medium heat, stirring constantly. Be very careful during this stage because if the level of heat rises and it starts to boil, the eggs will curdle. After about 20–25 minutes it will thicken as the eggs cook. Remove from the heat, discard the lime skin and allow the mixture to cool for about 30 minutes before adding the rum, bitters and essence.

Mix well, bottle and refrigerate.

Serve with freshly grated nutmeg.

Ponche de Crème

BEACH BUMS AND BOWMASTONS

Barbados, like any other tourist destination, has a number of friendly people who hang around the beach and make their living by befriending tourists. To a few of our visitors these guys are a godsend, providing various types of services which guarantee an enjoyable holiday. The rest of the population do not hold them in the same high regard and commonly refer to them as 'beach bums'.

Since a lot of time is spent on the beach waiting for eligible ladies to prey on, they usually become quite friendly with the bartenders in the area. When they get thirsty, they quite often order a Bowmaston. To anyone listening, this sounds like an exotic drink; however, Bowmaston is the name of a water pumping station and a Bowmaston is simply a drink of water usually served with a squeeze of lime and aromatic bitters and, depending on who needs to be impressed, a dash of nutmeg with a cherry floating on top.

SIMPLE SYRUP

INGREDIENTS
1¼ cups water
3 cups granulated sugar
1 tsp lemon juice

METHOD
Dissolve the sugar in the water and stir in the lemon juice. Heat to just about boiling point. Turn off the heat immediately, thus stopping the syrup from crystallising. Allow it to cool before using.

SORREL DRINK

This drink was once made only at Christmas-time. However, now that sorrel is dried commercially and available almost all year round we can enjoy this refreshing Caribbean drink at any time. It is also bottled commercially and sold in supermarkets.

INGREDIENTS

7 lb sorrel

sugar *to taste*

20 whole cloves

the peel from 2 whole oranges

2 oz fresh ginger *minced*

METHOD

Wash and remove the seeds from the fruit. Place all the ingredients in a large jar and pour in enough hot water to cover. Leave to stand for 24 hours, then strain.

Sweeten to taste, bottle and refrigerate.

Serve cold.

Sorrel Drink (with Caribbean Rum Cake)

SORREL LIQUEUR

Sorrel is a traditional Christmas drink. It is made from the sorrel fruit which is in season around November and December. In recent years the fruit has been available year-round because it is being dried on a commercial basis.

INGREDIENTS

4 lb sorrel

1 pt gin

1 cup rum

2 pts simple syrup

METHOD

Wash the sorrel and remove the seeds. Place the sorrel, rum and gin in a jar and leave for one week.

Next, remove the sorrel from the liquid and add the syrup.

Store in bottles for at least two weeks before serving – two months would be even better.

PINA COLADA

No vacation to the Caribbean would be complete without a few of these under your belt . . .

INGREDIENTS

½ cup rum

1 cup coconut cream

1 cup pineapple juice

3 cups crushed ice

pineapple wedges and maraschino cherries *for garnishing*

Serves 2

METHOD

Place all of the ingredients (except the pineapple wedges and cherries) in a blender and process for 30 seconds.

Pour into tall, chilled glasses and garnish with pineapple and cherries.

Pina Colada

NATIVE TREASURES

Caribbean cooking is as colourful as the many tropical fruits which abound in these beautiful islands. Not a day goes by when there is not some tasty fruit in season.

Native Treasures

Over the years, with each culture contributing its own fruits, vegetables, cooking techniques and, of course, peppers, to the pot, Caribbean cooking has slowly evolved into the hot, spicy and very tasty fare that we have come to enjoy so much.

But it is in the area of sauces and condiments that the true creativity of our people was highlighted. Using the many tropical fruits that abound in these beautiful islands they found imaginative ways to marry the old traditions with the new to 'keep the fire going'.

Just about anyone can prepare the great tasting recipes in this book, but it takes our *Native Treasures Sauces* to really make them come alive !

Bassa Bassa Sauce – a zesty combination of tamarinds, garlic and spices, blended to create the ultimate garlic lover's delight.

In Barbados to be involved in a 'Bassa Bassa' means to have the equivalent of a lover's quarrel. It is sour, sweet and spicy, and the making up is the best part of all. Our sauce brings forth all of these sensations, hence its name.

Bassa Bassa can be used as:
- a condiment to accompany seafood, poultry, pork, beef, potatoes, French fries, sausages, rice and pasta,
- basting sauce in the oven,
- relish for hot dogs and hamburgers,
- a dip for vegetables, cold cuts and chips,
- Bar-B-Q sauce on the grill,
- an excellent alternative to Tartar Sauce when mixed with mayonnaise,
- shrimp cocktail sauce,
- a dip for savoury starters (saltfish cakes, conch fritters, phulouri, etc).

Tamangy Chutney – a mild, tropical blend of tangy tamarinds, mangoes and the Barbados Scotch Bonnet pepper making a truly original chutney.

Tamangy can be used as:

- a condiment to accompany seafood, poultry, pork, beef, eggs, French fries, sausages, potatoes, rice and pasta,
- a salad dressing,
- relish for hot dogs and hamburgers,
- as a unique hors d'oeuvre poured over cream cheese and served with crackers,
- a spread on top of cheddar cheese in a sandwich,
- stir-fry sauce for vegetables,
- a dip for vegetables, cold cuts and chips.

Tropical Inferno – a hot, spicy blend of the Barbados Scotch bonnet pepper and exotic fruit (carambola or star fruit) create a unique sauce full of flavour.

For those who like the heat level a little higher, Tropical Inferno has developed a devoted following.
Tropical Inferno can be used as:

- a condiment to accompany seafood, poultry, pork, beef, sausages, eggs, potatoes, rice and pasta,
- added zest when cooking stews, seafood and meat dishes,
- a dip for savoury starters (saltfish cakes, phulouri, conch fritters, etc).

Kaiso Karamba Star Fruit Sauce – fruity, with just a hint of the Barbados Scotch bonnet pepper, this sauce is great on anything from seafood to pasta.

Kaiso Karamba can be used as:

- a relish for hot dogs and hamburgers,
- a condiment to accompany seafood, poultry, pork, beef, sausages, eggs, potatoes, rice and pasta,
- a dip for savoury starters (saltfish cakes, phulouri, conch fritters, etc),
- a unique hors d'oeuvre poured over cream cheese and served with crackers,
- a spread on top of cheddar cheese in a sandwich,
- a dip for vegetables and cold cuts.

Visit our home on the worldwide web at http://www.native-treasures.com

INDEX